Responses to 101 Questions on the Biblical Torah

REFLECTIONS ON THE PENTATEUCH

Roland E. Murphy, O. Carm.

PAULIST PRESS
New York/Mahwah, N.J.

Cover designs for this series are by James Brisson Design & Production, Williamsville, Vermont

The transliteration of Hebrew words is made in a simplified form for the sake of readers' pronunciation.

Copyright © 1996 by The Society of Mount Carmel
(Carmelite Fathers)

Library of Congress Cataloging-in-Publication Data

Murphy, Roland Edmund, 1917-
    Responses to 101 questions on the biblical Torah : reflections on the Pentateuch / Roland E. Murphy.
        p.   cm.
    Includes index.
    ISBN 0-8091-3630-9 (alk. paper)
        1. Bible. O.T. Pentateuch—Introductions. I. Title.
BS1225.2.M87 1996   95-50612
222'.106—dc20   CIP

Published by Paulist Press
997 Macarthur Boulevard
Mahwah, NJ 07430

Printed and bound in the
United States of America

CONTENTS

EXODUS/SHEMOTH

DEUTERONOMY/DEBARIM

TORAH AND NEW TESTAMENT

DEDICATED TO THE FACULTY, STAFF, AND STUDENTS OF
THE WASHINGTON THEOLOGICAL UNION

LIST OF ABBREVIATIONS

ABD   *Anchor Bible Dictionary*

ANET   *Ancient Near Eastern Texts* (J.B. Pritchard, ed.)

ET   English Translation

HBC   *Harper's Bible Commentary*

JPS   Jewish Publication Society of America

KJ   *Kings James Version*

LXX   Septuagint

NAB   *New American Bible*

NJBC   *New Jerome Biblical Commentary* (R.E. Brown, et al. eds.)

NCE   *New Catholic Encyclopedia*

NIB   *New Interpreter's Bible*

NJV   *New Jewish Version (the TaNaKH)*

NRSV   *New Revised Standard Version*

PREFACE

This little book will be of interest primarily to Christians. In general, Jews have their own questions about the Torah. In fact, they have raised thousands of questions in their rich exegetical tradition. A short introduction to this Jewish interpretation of the Torah can be found in the five volumes of the JPS (Jewish Publication Society) Torah Commentary, of which four have already been published, written by N. Sarna (Genesis, Exodus), B. Levine (Leviticus) and J. Milgrom (Numbers). My experience has been mainly with Christian audiences, and hence the concern has been more with questions that I have heard and answers I have formulated. But there are some lovely Jewish traditions that set the tone for the reverence with which the Christian should read the Torah. The most fetching is the portrait of God and the heavenly court, or angels, studying the Torah in the heavenly yeshivah (cf. Baba Mesi'a, 86a). Another is the tradition that Rabban Johanan ben Zakkai is said to have received in the tradition from Hillel and Shammai. "If you have studied much Torah, claim no special merit for yourself. It was for this that you were created" (cf. Avot, 2:9).

What happens when oral questions and answers are reduced to writing? There is a kind of change in genre. The answer may retain something of the original air of spontaneity, but not fully. The purpose of the question/answer is shifted when put in writing, in book form. The purpose of the writing is not merely to "answer," but to persuade the reader to go to the Bible and to read the text. Hence I have given many references to chapter and verse that would normally be absent in oral delivery. It can hardly be expected that a lecturer would have so many references ready at hand. But these have been supplied so that readers can verify for themselves in the text the basis for the answers that are given.

The questions discussed in this book are only a fraction of possible topics that actually come up for discussion in classes and public lectures. A selection has been made with an eye to presenting a rounded view of each book. Furthermore, the decision was made that Christians should ponder the significance of the Torah not only for the Jewish community but for themselves. Hence the last several questions depart from the topic, but only slightly, in order to explore the relationship between the Testaments, and to examine the Torah in the early Church.

THE 101 QUESTIONS AND RESPONSES

Q. 1. What is the meaning of the word "Torah"?

This is a Hebrew word with several meanings. It is used to designate the first five books of the Hebrew Scriptures, the so-called "Pentateuch," consisting of Genesis, Exodus, Leviticus, Numbers and Deuteronomy. In Jewish tradition each of these books has its own name, derived from the first word(s) of the book in question. The following pages indicate this by the divisions of the material to be discussed. Thus, Genesis/Bereshith. The first term, while customary in English, is really derived from the Greco-Latin tradition, and it means "origins" or "beginning." The Septuagint (abbreviated LXX, the oldest translation of the Bible from Hebrew into Greek) set the tone for this usage by employing the terms Genesis, Exodus, etc. *Bereshith* means "in the beginning." It is the first word of the book—indeed, of the Bible. Torah has become the name given to the first part of the Hebrew Scriptures, which is divided into three parts: Law, Prophets and Writings. An acronym, derived from the first letters of the Hebrew names (Torah, Nevi'im, Kethuvim) is Tanakh, the title of the new English translation published by the Jewish Publication Society in 1988.

In addition, there is the oral Torah. This is the interpretation of the biblical Torah that Jews believe was also revealed to Moses, and which was transmitted orally until it was gradually set down in writing during the Christian era in the works called Mishna and Talmud. The Torah, both in its written (biblical) form and in its oral (talmudic) form, is considered valid and binding for the rabbinic Judaism that prevails today.

In theological language the phrase "Law and Gospel" is frequently used as a kind of shorthand to indicate distinctive differences between the two Testaments. The distinction between the two terms has been popular in Protestant theology, but it may have outlived its usefulness. The distinction is too facile in that it summarizes the entire Hebrew Bible in such a way as to suggest that its main ingredient is law, and an aura of legalism is conjured up. As used here, Torah/Law designates the first five books of the Bible, unless otherwise noted.

It should be emphasized that Torah has other meanings. Basically, it means teaching or instruction, whether this teaching comes from God through Moses, or from a parent (cf. Prov 10:1). Thus, cultic instructions, ritual prescriptions, "statutes and ordinances" (cf. Deut 6:1) and many other regulations can be conveniently grouped under the "codes" that modern scholars find in the Torah, such as the "code of the covenant" (Ex 20:22–23:33). In many passages it serves as a compendium for Israel's life style, as in Deuteronomy 4:8: "…what great nation is there that has statutes and ordinances as just as this whole law?" Similarly, Jeremiah 31:31–33 speaks of a new covenant, when the Lord will put the law into his people, writing it upon their hearts.

Israel's understanding of the Torah is perhaps best appreciated in the book of Psalms. Psalm 1 speaks of "meditating" (reading aloud, poring over the text) on the law day and night. Psalm 19:7–10 hails the perfection of the law. The longest of the psalms (Ps 119) has twenty-two strophes of eight lines each, following the sequence of the Hebrew alphabet (i.e., an "acrostic" psalm), and using synonyms for law, instruction, statutes, etc. in each line. The law is hailed as a joy, as life-giving, more precious than all possessions. One gathers from such prayers the deep happiness and rapture that the knowledge of God's will provided for the faithful; see, for example, 119:17, 25, 47, etc. One of the high points of a synagogue service is the carrying of the Torah scroll among the community. Many Jews today celebrate a feast called *simchat Torah*, "the joy of the Torah."

In contrast to the rich aura that surrounds the term "Torah" stands the dry and formidable synonym customary in Christian circles, "Pentateuch." It comes from the Greek words meaning "five" and "container." The latter word came to refer to the written leather or papyrus scrolls that were preserved in these receptacles. The codex or "book" form for writing material did not begin until the early Christian era. You will find that biblical studies have complicated the situation by referring to "Tetrateuch," the first four books, Genesis to Numbers, and also to "Hexateuch," the first six books of the Bible, Genesis to Joshua. Behind the terminology are certain views about the interpretation of this material.

Q. 2. How is the Torah structured?

Almost any literary composition can be outlined or structured in several ways, depending on the principle of division that one is using. If one follows the story line, as it were, the following structure of the Torah can be proposed:

Genesis 1–11, the pre-history

Genesis 12–50, the story of the patriarchs, and Joseph and his brothers

Exodus 1–19, the story of the exodus from Egypt

Exodus 19:1–Numbers 10:11, the events of Sinai until the departure about a year later

Numbers 11:1–22:1, the journey through the wilderness to Transjordan

Numbers 22:2–36:13, the events in the plains of Moab

Deuteronomy: this book is best structured by the recognition of three major speeches of Moses: 1:6–4:40; 5:1–28:69; 29:1–32:52. These are indicated by references to Moses' addressing the people. The last chapters contain the Song of Moses, his "final" blessing, and the story of his death on Mount Nebo.

Thus the story line goes from the creation of the world to the patriarchs, to the descendants who were freed from slavery under the leadership of Moses, and who entered into a covenant with *yhwh* and bound themselves to the stipulations of the covenant. The journey brings the descendants of Joseph from Egypt to Sinai and on to the plains of Moab. Just at this point you might wonder: Why did the Torah/Pentateuch stop here (with the death of Moses the last item recorded, Deuteronomy 34)? The thrust of the narrative, even from the time of Abraham, has been the promise of a land. But the Pentateuch ends with the people just on the verge of the promised land. The natural continuation and terminus of the story line is the book of Joshua that relates the possession of the land under Joshua, and the settlement there (one would then speak of a Hexateuch, or six books). Why did the Torah end where it ended? Why were these five books considered a separate unit when the story calls out for the climax of the gift of the land in Joshua? One can only guess at the answer. James Sanders has provided an attractive explanation. When the Torah received its final form in the immediate post-exilic period, there was a desire to stress fidelity to the law of Moses. The tribulations of the exile (587–539) were due to Israel's infidelity to the Torah. Since the first five books contained the manifestation of God's will in the sweep of text that goes from Exodus 19 to Numbers 10, as well as in the Deuteronomic laws that are preached so fervently in Deuteronomy 12–26, and since Moses was the lawgiver par excellence, it made good sense for the people to return to these "origins" and to live by them in the post-exilic period. Moses became the hero for a people who interpreted their downfall as a failure to hear the word of God. Israel now had another chance. As Psalm 95:7 puts it. "If today you would hear his voice…" The constant repetition of "today" throughout Deuteronomy returned the people to Sinai (and Moab) in spirit to renew the covenant with the Lord and pledge fidelity.

Q. 3. Did Moses write the Torah?

The shortest and true answer is NO, but it calls for much explanation. If Moses did not write it, who did? How did this work come into existence? What can be said about the Mosaic authorship of the Pentateuch? For centuries it was an accepted fact that he did write the first five books, but in the medieval period it was asked how he could write about his own death (Deuteronomy 34). Today many still hold to Mosaic authorship of the Pentateuch. However, there are serious objections to this view. One of the first indications that appeared in careful study of the Pentateuch was the recognition of different names for the divinity. Thus, some parts preferred the sacred name, *yhwh*, and others the generic name for God, *elohim*. The differences were deeper than a mere variation in the use of these names. With the variation went a certain style and viewpoint, idiomatic expressions peculiar to each, so that the respective parts were termed Yahwist and Elohist. These were represented by the letter J (in German Y is rendered by J) and E. Further investigation led to the recognition of a priestly source (called P), and there was also Deuteronomy (D). This view of the division of the Pentateuch became common over the last two centuries and has been associated with one of its major proponents, Julius Wellhausen (d. 1919).

Many variations have developed, both as to the dating (late, or as early as David/Solomon for J) and as to the nature of the four sources: Were they written documents, or were supplements added to a given source? Today there is a tendency to eliminate the E tradition, and also to delay the writing of the final form of the Pentateuch to the post-exilic period. These various views point to the hypothetical character of any neat picture of the formation of the Pentateuch. Certainly, there was a development over the centuries, but details on dating and also on combinations are difficult to ascertain. Readers will find it advantageous to recognize the general validity of the distinction of sources. This enables them to understand the appearances of doublets, in which basically the same event is related twice—e.g., the endangerment of Sarah (Gen 12:10–31; 20:1–18; cf. 26:6–11). It should also be noted that readers will be struck by different emphases within the work; the predilection of P for genealogies and for matters of worship; the fervent language and viewpoints that characterize D, and so forth. A detailed but clear explanation of the arguments in favor of the four sources is laid out by R.E. Friedman in *ABD* VI, 605–22. A careful analysis of the formation of the Pentateuch is exceedingly helpful. It makes for an interesting close reading of the various books. Even a superficial reading of the Pentateuch reveals many different literary forms: ancient poems, liturgical prayers and actions, family histories, victory songs, and several codes of law that understandably differ with each other (law is naturally flexible according to changing conditions). It is fair to conclude from this that the oral and written traditions that were finally encoded in the Torah came from many persons and places. Many translations are provided with annotations that help the reader by suggesting the identity of the sources (e.g., the annotations to the *NRSV* in the *New Oxford Annotated Bible*).

From what has been said it is clear that any answer concerning the "authorship" of the Pentateuch is a complicated one, and that more than one hypothesis has been advanced to explain its present form. One might ask another question: Does all this analysis yield real profit? Why not consider the Pentateuch as a whole? After all, there never existed a J source by itself that was considered to be *biblical*. The same is true of the other portions of the work. It is the final form of the Torah that counts and that was accepted as Bible by both Jews and Christians. This holistic approach to the Torah has been underscored by the research of Brevard Childs (*The Interpretation of the Old Testament as Scripture* [Minneapolis: Fortress, 1979]). This is a useful reminder that carving up the Torah often yields only hypothetical building blocks for the final work. It is a wise caution against the extremes that have been reached in analyzing the Pentateuch. At the same time, there is a value in recognizing the distinctive viewpoints or "theologies" within the entire work; they have not been swallowed up in the final form of the Torah and are deserving of due consideration.

Q. 4. If Torah means instruction or law, how can it be applied to books that contain so much of the historical traditions of Israel?

We have seen that the name "Torah" given to these books is simply an historical fact. We can only speculate as to the reasons that may have led to this designation. One obvious reason is that the legal portions of the Torah extend from Exodus 25–40 through the book of Leviticus up to Numbers 10. In addition there is the Deuteronomic law in Deuteronomy 12–26. Merely from the point of view of content, this abundant legislation would justify the name. Second, we may point to the consideration advanced above in Q. 2: the story line seems not to have appeared as important as the role of Moses as mediator and lawgiver. Moreover, there are important theological associations made between the non-legal and legal sections. Thus, two reasons are given for the observance of the sabbath. The first states that after creation the Lord rested on the sabbath, blessing and consecrating it (Ex 20:8–11). So no work is to be done on that day. However, it is specified in Deuteronomy 5:14–16 that no work is to be done on the sabbath, even by one's own slaves, because Israel is to keep in mind that they were once slaves in Egypt, and were saved only "by the mighty hand and outstretched arm" of the Lord.

Q. 5. Is the Torah more important than the "Prophets" and the "Writings" that form the rest of the Hebrew Bible?

As indicated above in Q. 1, the Jewish canon is tripartite, and the picturesque acronym for the Bible takes the first (Hebrew) letters of the three parts (T, N, K) and forms the word Tanakh (also Tenach and other variants). From an historical point of view, it seems clear that the Torah was completed ahead of the prophetic corpus, and that the Writings were still open in the intertestamental period (e.g., the inclusion of the book of Daniel among them after 165 B.C.).

The Torah is more important, in the sense of being more foundational for the Jewish people than other parts of the Bible. This claim is evident from the statements and writings of Jews today, as well as from the role that the Torah has played in history. It is significant to observe that there is an oral Torah to accompany the biblical Torah, but there is no oral tradition that accompanies the Prophets and the Writings. The latter portions are indeed important and the Bible cannot do without them, but they are simply not on the same level with the Torah. It is what I would call the foundational character of "the books of Moses" that makes them so central to Jewish identity. This importance was confirmed early on by the development of the oral tradition that eventually came to be recorded separately. It is appropriate here to flesh out what is meant by this oral tradition.

The following table will provide at a glance the final written expression of the oral torah. Basically this is contained in several writings of Jewish rabbis that were completed by the seventh century C.E.:

Mishna: Oral torah from the time of Moses, collected about 200 C.E. by Judah the Prince (*nasi*), consisting of theoretical narrative (haggadah) and practical rules (halakah). There are six divisions of sixty-two tractates.

Tosefta: A supplement or commentary on the Mishna (and about four times as large as the material it complements), dated to about 300 C.E.

Talmud: There are two of these—that of Palestine (also known as Yerushalmi, put in writing about 400 C.E.), and that of Babylonia (also known as Bavli, dated to about 600 B.C.). The Talmud contains the full and authoritative expression of the Judaism we know today.

There are, of course, other types of Jewish literature, such as the *Midrash*. This is a biblical commentary on the Bible, as it were—or "writing with Scripture," as J. Neusner has put it. And the Jewish commentators of the Middle Ages are justly famous. But the above classification constitutes the heart of the Judaism of the dual Torah. For further details, see the *Introduction to Rabbinic Literature* (New York: Doubleday, 1994) by J. Neusner.

GENESIS/BERESHITH

Q. 6. How is the book of Genesis structured?

The pre-history, Genesis 1–11
The period of the patriarchs, 12–36
The story of Joseph, 37–50

There are various ways of outlining a book, but these three major divisions may be more helpful than many details. Perhaps it is worth mentioning that the major portion of the patriarchal period is occupied by Jacob since he includes almost all of the Joseph story within his lifetime. Isaac is represented only fleetingly, almost as a mirror image of his father, and figures largely only in chapters 26–27. Even the famous *akedah* or "binding of Isaac" (Genesis 22) seems to be part of the Abraham story (chapters 12–25).

Another way of dividing Genesis is to follow the signs left by the priestly tradition: the appearance of the word *toledoth*, or "generations," which is found ten times. It has various functions. It will introduce a genealogy sometimes by way of an historical summary or as a correlation of individuals and generations to each other (e.g., 5:1; 10:1; 11:10; 25:12; 35:1). It is also used to introduce a new section of narrative (e.g, Gen 2:4; 6:9; 11:27; 25:19; 37:2). The customary formula is: "these are the generations of so and so," and they are easy to recognize. The formula is used only a few times outside of Genesis (e.g., Ex 6:14).

Q. 7. If history began with creation, how can you call the first chapters of Genesis "pre-history"?

Your question really has several parts. The first is the supposition that history began with creation. What began with creation is the existence of various kinds of life, and we really have no knowledge of these beginnings. Scientists speak of the origins of the universe in terms of the "Big-Bang" theory, and many regard it as scientifically respectable and at least in harmony with what we know from Genesis. But this is beside the point; we are not interested in comparing scientific theory with the biblical data. What should be said is that history had not yet begun even after God created humans. They lived and had experiences but have left no trace of this. History begins when some kind of record of living things, whether written or unwritten, is left by them. Later generations analyze these records or artifacts in order to construct the history of a period. Obviously, nothing has come down to us from the "beginnings" related in Genesis 1–11.

"Pre-history" is merely a convenient term used by biblical students to indicate the peculiar nature of the incidents related in Genesis 1–11. They are not history as we know the term. Rather they are interpretations of reality: the nature of the relationship between God and the world, especially all living beings (humans being the climax), the failure of humans to respond to God's offer of life, as exemplified by the story of the flood, and further by the story of the tower of Babel. It is when the narrative begins to talk about ancient cities, and the migration of Abraham to the land of Canaan, that one enters into an area that is subject to some historical control.

Other terms have been used to describe the nature of the events related in Genesis 1–11, such as myth or imaginative writings. These terms tend to be shocking to those who have preconceived ideas about what is related in these chapters. Often there is the reaction: then you are saying that what is related here is not true, not historical. Not at all; one is not saying this. What one is saying is that history and truth are not identical terms. There are other kinds of truth besides history. Certainly that is something we can agree upon. What is the "truth" of a metaphor, of a parable, of a psalm, of a love song, of a short story? One could go on and on. It is first incumbent upon a reader of the Bible to be aware of the type of literature that he or she is reading. Is it history or creative poetry? Moreover one must examine the criteria one is using for the classification of history. All historical writing is interpretive, and are we sure of the author's intention? Would the author be writing satire under the cloak of history (one thinks of the book of Jonah)? History is an art that has grown and improved considerably over the centuries. The standards that are set for writing history by the guild of present-day historians were not known in former days, and we cannot expect that the biblical writers be held to such standards. We must take the text as it stands, with all the limitations of the time of its composition. The biblical writings were not destined for us in the first place, but for the readers of biblical times. It would have been impossible for them to understand the divine message if it had come forth in the King James version of Holy Writ, or some equivalent, reflecting the presuppositions of our day. This issue of history can be defined and discussed forever; the best approach is to read the biblical text, holding in abeyance the modern pre-conceptions we bring to it. Or to put it another way, we must recognize the limitations of ancient texts, if they can be called limitations, and allow ourselves to be taught by them without imposing our standards of history upon them.

One issue that will probably provide wonderment and disbelief is the extremely long life span of people recorded in these chapters. Perhaps one of the best known "facts" is that the oldest person was Methuselah who is said to have lived 969 years (Gen 5:27). He forms part of the generation of people living before the flood, and all of them live to an incredible number of years. Readers have to ask themselves the meaning of this. These numbers become more intelligible when we discover that there are similar lists in Babylonian and Sumerian records that have several heroes in the period before the flood, and these also live out a fantastic number of years. One can notice in the biblical data that there is a steady decrease in the life span of the individuals who are listed. There is no certain interpretation of the intent behind these numbers. They seem to belong to myth (the oldest life span in the Sumerian list is seventy-two thousand years). At least one can say that these genealogies have the function of filling in the time before the flood. Along with the table of nations in chapter 10 they serve to provide some kind of continuity to the narrative. Theologically this is a statement that the Lord created the entire world, and the tradition made whatever use it could of the available genealogies and lists.

I have just mentioned the flood, and perhaps you are thinking about the historicity of the account recorded in chapters 6–8. Did the flood described there really occur? No, because *that* description is really the creation of two sources, P and J. See Q. 11 for more details. Each source had its own version of a flood, and the two have been put together to form a loose unity that exemplifies the spread of sin in the world (Gen 6:5–7,11–12), and the punishment it deserves. It is for this reason that the writers made use of the flood stories that were so prominent in the ancient world (see Q. 9).

Q. 8. Is the creation "story" in Genesis the same as "creationism"?

No, it is not. First let us examine the portrayal of creation in Genesis 1. It is really an impressive chapter, attributed to the priestly tradition. There is a certain magnificence in the way in which the actions and words are coordinated. God speaks, and something happens. Then a verdict of "goodness" follows. It should be noted that Genesis 1:1 is translated in various ways. The time-honored rendition followed the Septuagint understanding, "In the beginning...." But it is also possible to render as many modern versions do, "When God began to create...the earth was...." What follows is described according to the understanding of the world as the author (and the readers) understood it to be at the time. The blue firmament that stretched from one horizon to the other was placed to separate the waters above (where the Lord dwelt with his heavenly court) from the waters below. The work of separation of things has begun, and there is the consistent repetition of the verdict that "it was good." In addition, this follows the sequence of day one, day two, etc. All is described as an effortless work of the Lord who merely speaks, and things happen. After the first three days (and each day seems to be understood as it appears to human experience, with an evening and morning), the work of populating what has been separated begins—an artificial arrangement that was already noted as long ago as Thomas Aquinas. On it goes until the Lord comes to a climactic moment (Gen 1:26) when there is a consultation with the heavenly court, the "sons of God," who praise and serve him (cf. Ps 29; Is 6): "Let us make human beings in our image"—*our* image, that is also the likeness of God: "male and female he created them." They are made in the image of God, i.e., they somehow share in the divine dominion over all creation, and are blessed with fertility (1:28). All creation was pronounced good, and so God rested on the seventh day, the holy day of the sabbath.

This stirring narrative has been cheapened by ridicule, such as how was there light on the first day, when the sun was created only on the fourth day—a question that goes back to the time of Origen (d. circa 254) at least! This and similar questions are not on target because they fail to recognize the specific literary form used by the author. This is not an eye-witness account of the *mode* of creation; rather it registers the fact of creation, and all neatly disposed according to the way in which the Israelite operated in the ancient world: working for six days and resting on the seventh in obedience to the Lord's command.

As if to confound any literalist interpretation of Genesis 1, there is another view of creation in Genesis 2 (usually attributed to the Yahwist, or J) that puts creation in another light. This story is centered more on human beings. The earth is there but untilled, so the Lord God forms a male out of the dust of the earth (an "adam" from the "adamah" as the Hebrew puts it), and blows the breath of life into it so that it is a living being. Note that there is no concept of body/soul, such as we are used to; a human is breathed-upon matter. The Lord God decides to provide him with company ("not good for man to be alone"). But all the animals that are made do not really offer companionship, so the Lord God creates the woman—how else, in order to show that she has the same nature as the man?—from his side. The rhapsodic discovery of the man—"bone of my bones," etc.—indicates admiration for the divine achievement. It is important to note how two creation stories have been freely juxtaposed by a person (a later editor?) who sees no reason to rank one higher than the other. They are both "true." There is no compulsion to say, "Well, this is how it really happened." There is a comfortable ability in the ancient writings to live with such ignorance about the manner, as long as the important things are clearly described: divine intervention, the creation of all, and the special effort that went into the making of the man and the woman.

Creationism, and there are many forms of it, does not have such a relaxed attitude toward the doctrine of creation as the Bible presents. Genesis gives us two imaginative presentations, but creationism in its drive for a literal understanding cannot be satisfied until it has snapped a picture of the divine activity it claims to see described in the text. Basically, one can sum up the case (even if more arguments can be mounted) in two statements. (1) There is in the Bible no single portrayal of the creative activity of God. In fact, there are presentations in other books of the Bible that differ from the Genesis accounts (e.g., Ps 89:5–11). (2) It follows from this that it is incumbent upon the reader to shed previous convictions, if necessary, and to allow oneself to be drawn into the level of the text, as simple but complex as it is.

Q. 9. Are there other creation stories in the ancient Near East that can be compared with the Genesis narrative?

Indeed there are. Three works in particular are important to read as background to the narrative in Genesis 1–11. Perhaps the most famous of these is the *Enuma Elish* ("When on high"), which has been called the Babylonian epic of creation, and dated to about 1200 B.C. However, it is not really concerned with creation; it is the story of how Marduk became the chief god of the Babylonian pantheon. In the course of his ascendancy he defeats the goddess Tiamat (related to "sea") in a mighty battle and creates the world out of her carcass. A certain minor divinity, Kingu, had aided her, and Marduk sees to it that he is slain and humankind is formed out of his blood. The function of human beings is to serve the gods. When this work was first published in 1876 it created a great stir because of its superficial similarity with Genesis 1, and it also contained other parallels to the Bible. It should be read and understood for its own sake (translation available in *ANET*, 60–72). The story borrows several elements from other works.

One of these is the myth of *Atrahasis*; it was famous as containing a flood story, and discoveries in this century have turned up a fuller account. It is a story of the relationship of gods among themselves and with human beings. At the start there is a division among the gods: those who rest and lesser gods who work to provide them with what they need. This leads to a revolt and the result is compromise. The ringleader among the rebels is slain and his blood is mixed with clay, and a human race comes into existence: seven males and seven females. Their function is to till fields and thus provide provisions for the gods. However, this solution is short-lived. These humans raise such a hue and cry that Enlil, king of the gods, can get no sleep. Punitive measures (plague, famine, etc.) are of no avail. A huge flood is decreed, but one of the gods reveals this to Atrahasis (the name means "very wise") and suggests a boat to save himself, his household and animals. After the flood, sacrifice is offered to the gods (cf. Gen 8:20–21). The final result of all this is not clear from the text, but if one can judge from the parallel in the Gilgamesh epic, Atrahasis and his wife become immortal, but not so their descendants. However, the "noise" that caused all the trouble in the first place is removed. Several interpretations of the Atrahasis story have been offered, e.g., that its concern was the overpopulation of the earth. Be that as it may, it certainly deals with the punishment (by flood) of the human race, and the story of the flood comes to be taken up and inserted in a third great ancient Mesopotamian work, the epic of *Gilgamesh*.

This epic is a patchwork of early tales from Mesopotamian lore about an apparently real king of Uruk in the first half of the first millennium B.C. It is a classic and deserves to be read for its own sake (*ANET*, 72–99). Here we merely wish to highlight some of the parallels it shares with the Genesis text. In its final form (an Assyrian rendition of about the seventh century) we can read the story of Gilgamesh's search for immortality. This is a paramount concern after the death of Enkidu with whom he had shared so many adventures. He goes in search of a certain Utnapishtim and his wife (this man was known as Ziusudra in the earlier Sumerian version of the flood) who had become immortal after the flood—the biblical Noah. He is warned by a servant girl that his search is doomed, that the gods have apportioned death as the human lot— hence he should enjoy the simple things of life such as dancing and playing, and the joys of family life. But this realistic advice is lost upon him, and he stays his course till he finds the survivors of the flood. From them he learns the story of the flood and of the gift of immortality. But the warning of the servant girl comes true: Gilgamesh is unable to stay awake; sleep (symbolic of death) overcomes him. Finally Utnapishtim reveals to him a plant that will secure his immortality. Unfortunately, when Gilgamesh stops to bathe in a pool, a serpent steals the plant!

The broad similarity between the above highlights of the Mesopotamian myths and the pre-history in Genesis 1–11 is fairly obvious. But one should be cautious in attempting to explain just how the biblical tradition incorporated this world into its own understanding. It is unlikely that the biblical writer(s) would have had copies of various cuneiform texts (wedge-shaped writing, in which these texts were written) and simply transferred them into the biblical narrative. No, it is far more likely that these myths circulated broadly and orally in the culture of the Fertile Crescent, and that they became known to the Hebrews. When the latter came to express their understanding of creation and the human situation, they were doubtless influenced by these stories. They found them fruitful for their own reflections upon reality, and they expressed them according to their own genius and beliefs.

It would be a mistake to limit this mythical style of thinking only to the first chapters of Genesis. It runs through much of biblical poetry. For example, creation is portrayed as a battle with the powers of chaos, personified in Sea, in Leviathan, and in Rahab, in various passages. Thus we read in Psalm 74:13–14,

> You stirred the Sea by your might.
> You smashed the heads of the Dragons on the waters.
> You crushed the heads of Leviathan…(cf. also Ps 89:9–12).

We learn from Isaiah 27:1 that Leviathan is a seven-headed monster, and from Psalm 104:26 that it is the Lord's plaything, but not for humans to play with (Job 40:25–42). Scholars have come up with a neat German term for this theme: *Chaoskampf*—God's battle with chaos. The divine power destroys chaos in creating and preserving creation.

Q. 10. How would you characterize Genesis 3 that relates the fall and punishment of the first parents?

This is the same genre of writing that we find in the creation stories. It is very imaginative; serpents don't speak to humans, nor do humans reply to them in animated conversation, and there is the always famous question of the Scopes trial of years ago as to the manner of a serpent's means of locomotion before being sentenced to "crawl." Such points draw a smile, but they obscure the high literary art in which temptation is described in this passage, how slowly but surely the woman is drawn into conversation and finishes by admiring the fruit and relishing the happy prospect associated with eating it. This is in fact a very subtle and artful text, marked by wordplay ("clever" and "naked" in 3:1 and 2:25 of the Hebrew text are the same word, '*arum*). This telling description of temptation mirrors universal human experience. The purpose of the chapter is to show that sin comes not from God, nor from the goodness of the creation, but from human beings. They do not trust the command of God, but listen to the fatal temptation "to be like God." What is the result? Not punishment. The curse is leveled at the serpent and the ground, not at the man and woman. The subtlety of the presentation makes one appreciate the malevolence of the serpent; it is an evil power that will be locked in struggle with humanity. Just as a person steps on a snake to crush its head, the heel is also vulnerable to the venom of the animal.

This so-called "protoevangelium" ("gospel before the gospel") has been too quickly referred to Christ (and, because of a faulty reading that crept into the Vulgate Latin, erroneously to Mary), but the immediate sense is the struggle of humans with evil. The words to the woman explain her ever-present situation: the inherent pain of child-bearing, and her current situation as one born into a patriarchal culture where the man rules. This is in lively contrast to her role as viewed in 1:27 and 2:22–24. The ground is cursed; it is an explanation giving the etiology of the ancient Near Eastern peasant who must struggle with the soil to make a living. Finally, the mortality of the couple who could have enjoyed the fruit of the tree of life (3:22, 24) is indicated by the final words, "to dust you shall return."

Needless to say, this famous passage is known to all, and is usually viewed in terms of original sin. But it should be emphasized that that phrase is not in the biblical text. Indeed, the Hebrew Bible does not again refer to this famous event in Genesis 3. Original sin is a later theological development, based on Romans 5 and especially on the theological explanation of St. Augustine (d. 430). The difficulty for moderns is that the depths of Pauline and Augustinian thought are really not understood, and their views are bowdlerized into a mechanical explanation. It is interesting to see how the development of dogma has affected the notion of original sin in modern theology (e.g., with the late Karl Rahner).

Q. 11. Would it be true to say that sin is the principal theme of the first chapters of the Bible, especially those about Noah and the flood?

I would not like to put it that way. After all, the opening lines deal with creation and with the divine generosity to humankind. And it doesn't fail. After the cursing of serpent and ground there is the touching note that the Lord God made garments of skins for Adam (this is the first time that the proper name appears) and his wife.

Yet it is true that sin is a major topic in these chapters. One reads immediately of murder in the first generation, the story of Cain and of Abel. The violence of Cain is reflected in his progeny, Lamech, who boasts of seventy-sevenfold vengeance (4:23). These evils are emphasized by the Lord's sorrow at having created humankind, and the ensuing resolution to destroy them as well as other living beings from the face of the earth (6:5–7). There is one exception: Noah.

The story of Noah need not be told here, but one cannot help wondering if readers appreciate the art with which the narrative has been composed. It is a masterful example of how two traditions have been woven together, the Yahwist and the Priestly versions. So smooth are the connections that only a careful reader will detect that more than one hand is at work. It is not just a case of the usual differences in the alternation of the names of God, but the style of presentation. P gives the exact times when the flood began and ended (7:11; 8:5), the dimensions of the ark, and the length of time that the flood lasts. In addition, there are some significant differences. For J seven pairs of clean animals and only one pair of each of the unclean animals (7:2–3) enter the ark, whereas in P one pair of each type enters (6:19–20; 7:15–16). For J the flood is a downpour of forty days, but in P the water appears to come from below as it rises for one hundred and fifty days and subsides for one hundred and fifty (7:24; 8:3). The two accounts do not agree with each other. P relates the famous "Noachic" covenant (9:12–17) that has been interpreted as referring to the Gentiles (although it seems to be a covenant with earth, not to destroy it and its inhabitants). There is a neat twist in establishing the rainbow (after the flood!) as the sign of the covenant. We have already referred to flood stories and heroes above in Q. 9. What relationship has the biblical story to those of the Fertile Crescent? There can be no question but that the biblical writers were aware of the other flood stories (whether orally or in written form). The sending out of the birds (8:6–12) and also the sacrifice after the deluge (8:20) reflect very specific details in the Gilgamesh rendition of the flood, and the general sequence of events is known to us also from the Atrahasis epic. The significant *difference* is the purpose of the flood in the biblical narrative; it is a punishment of sin. It has nothing to do with mere disturbance of the rest of the gods, nor with the prevention of over-population, etc. Such stories were surely current in Israel as well as in the rest of the Fertile Crescent, but the biblical narrative differs significantly from these by reason of the motivation that is stated.

It is an interesting fact that no story parallel to the tower of Babel has ever turned up in the Fertile Crescent. Yes, there is a tower of Babel, in the sense that the ziggurat, or temple tower, is a Mesopotamian creation, the most famous being named Etemenanki. The biblical narrative seems to be an etiology concerning such temples, how they came to be. Actually, more than one motif is present in this story of the tower of Babel. It illustrates the spread of humanity across the earth, and also scores its pride, symbolized in this tower that is sarcastically described as a building with its top in the heavens. Despite the intentions of humankind, this symbol of human pride turns out to be so puny that the Lord has to come down to see the city and the tower. In a neat wordplay the Lord "balals" (confuses) the language of the people of Babel, and they are scattered before they can achieve their goal, and their disunity is mirrored in all their various languages.

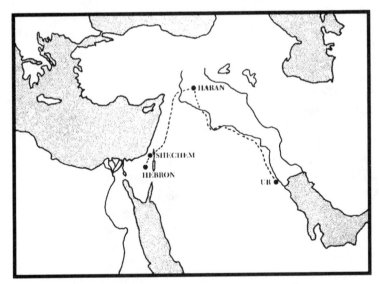

The Journey of Abraham from Ur to Canaan

Q. 12. How is Abraham connected with the "pre-history" of Genesis?

We have to back up a little to see this question in context. The biblical tradition wants to show the continuation of the human race after the flood, and so we have a table of nations in chapter 10 that reflects Israel's understanding of the neighbors inhabiting its world: the descendants of Shem, Ham and Japhet. After the story of the tower of Babel there is a line of the descendants of Shem that culminates in the birth of Abram and Nahor from Terah. They are situated in Ur (in the southern part of Mesopotamia) and then in Haran in northern Mesopotamia. An ominous note is sounded in 11:30: Sarai, wife of Abram, is sterile, a grave affliction in the biblical world—and Abram is stated to be seventy-five years old (12:4). Notice that the names of Abram and Sarai are not changed to Abraham and Sarah until Genesis 17:5.

This sets the stage for the abrupt command and promise that the Lord gives to Abram in 12:1–3. He is told to leave his country and relatives for an unnamed land "that I will show you." He is to become a great nation and achieve a great name (renown) and also be blessed in such a way by the Lord that he will be a blessing to the entire human race. This is meant to sound as lofty and also as preposterous as it really is. A great nation from a mother that is barren? This becomes a major theme in the Abraham story: the birth of an heir.

Abram's dwelling in the land of Canaan, promised to him and his offspring in 12:7, does not appear auspicious. He worships at venerable sanctuaries and reaches the desert land of the Negeb in the south, no stranger to famine conditions. The natural move now is to seek food and refuge in Egypt. Here we are introduced for the first time to the motif of Sarai's endangerment. She accedes to her husband's request to pose as his sister, lest the Egyptians slay him to acquire her because of her great beauty even at her age. Abram looks selfish and deceitful in this episode. But there is more involved than saving one's skin. The real issue is: What about the promise of an heir and nation? As the story unravels, Abram prospers but the (unnamed) pharaoh and the royal household are afflicted with plagues. At work in the narrative is the connection between suffering and wrongdoing. There must be an explanation for these disasters, and the pharaoh attributes them to his appropriation of Sarai. No matter that he did this unknowingly and had actually been deceived; the ancients saw a connection between the material deed and the result. Abram leaves Egypt richer then when he came to it. The biblical writers were not embarrassed to show the moral deficiencies of their ancestors. Abram can surely be faulted for such "gallant" conduct, but the deeper issue is that he does not show much concern about the promise.

One cannot leave this episode without considering its doublet in Genesis 20 (usually attributed to the Elohist tradition). There is only a slight change in the characters. The pharaoh is replaced by the king of Gerar (in the south, near later Philistia). But dialogue replaces action. There is a dialogue between God and King Abimelech in a dream. He is threatened with death because he has taken Sarah (recall that in 17:5 the names of the patriarch and his wife have been changed), and already his household has been afflicted with sterility (20:17–18). But the king challenges God: Does he slay innocent people? And he demonstrates his innocence by quoting Abraham's lie, the wife/sister pretense. God grants that point and claims that it is the reason why he has kept the king from even touching her. But now he must restore her to Abraham. The king faces down Abraham who comes up with his old excuse (even dating it from the time the couple had left for Canaan). The king is inexplicably generous, giving Abraham all kinds of riches and freeing Sarah. Then at the prayer of Abraham, a brazen liar, God removes the affliction from Abimelech and his household. Another puzzling story.

Q. 13. How many covenants did God make with Abraham?

There is really one covenant, and that is with Abraham and his descendants. I think your question is prompted by two similar chapters, 15 and 17, and the word for covenant (*berith*) occurs thirteen times in chapter 17. Chapter 15 really deals with promise, which is, of course, intrinsic to the covenant relationship that will be sealed in chapter 17. The word "covenant" designates an agreement or compact between parties, whether political or religious. For our purposes, we should note two kinds: covenants of divine promise (God binds self), and those of human obligation (e.g., the obligations of the Mosaic covenant). Chapter 15 describes two promises: of descendants and of land, and both go back to the initial words of the Lord to Abram in 12:1–3. Abram complains that he is still childless, that future prospects seem to lie with his servant,

Eliezer of Damascus, who will be the heir. To the contrary, the Lord assures him of an heir from his own loins, and many offspring that will rival the stars in number. Abram yields to the Lord's plan; in return God considers Abram's faith and trust as righteousness. That is what righteousness is: a relationship, the kind of openness to the Lord that marked Abram's attitude; he relied solely on the word of the Lord. Verse 6 is one of the most famous of biblical quotations because it is taken up by Paul in Romans 4:9, 22, and extended to belief in the One who raised Jesus from the dead. In 15:7–21 the subject of the promise is "this land," the fertile crescent from the river of Egypt (wadi El-Arish, south of Gaza) to the Euphrates. Abram asks for a sign (15:8), and in an elaborate and mysterious rite the Lord "cuts a covenant" (v. 18) with Abram, thus assuming the obligation of fulfilling the promise of a land.

In chapter 17, usually attributed to the priestly source, we have another portrayal of covenant and also the appearance of new names. The divinity appears to Abraham as "God Almighty" (*El Shaddai*, literally perhaps, "God, the One of the Mountain") and changes the name of Abram. This name seems to mean "Ab (father) is high." Abraham is interpreted as "father of a multitude." Sarai's name is changed to Sarah ("princess," v. 15). The covenant begins with the promise of a progeny, and becomes an "eternal" covenant with them: they are to occupy the land of promise. The sign of the covenant is circumcision, a practice that was known in the ancient world (but not adopted by all). It was only in the post-exilic period that it assumed for Israel the importance of being the covenantal sign; the priestly tradition traces it to the "father" of the people. Abraham's reaction to the blessing (of fertility given to Sarah and the announcement of a son) is at first blush astonishing: while he does obeisance, he also laughs at the idea of conception in their advanced ages. Instead of God's plan he proposes Ishmael as the child of promise (the son of Hagar, not Sarah), but in vain; the divine plan will be put into operation. Ishmael is not included, but he is not excluded from God's concern. He is to be blessed with a progeny, too. But the covenant is to be transmitted through Isaac.

Q. 14. What role does Lot play in the Abraham story?

I am inclined to say that Lot's role is out of all proportion to his importance. You may recall that he is Abraham's nephew (Gen 11:31) and comes to Canaan with him. When there is a quarrel between Abraham's servants and those of Lot (chap. 13), Abraham resolves the problem most generously. Lot can depart and settle where he pleases. He chooses the fertile Jordan area, while Abraham goes to Hebron. Abraham comes to his rescue when Lot is captured by invaders (the mysterious chapter 14), and Abraham rescues him. One gets the impression that Lot serves as a contrast with the noble Abraham. Once he settles in the "cities of the plain" (Gen 13:12), his course is all downhill. The unsavory story of the attempt of the Sodomites to maltreat the two men (angels, 19:1) who accept Lot's hospitality is the beginning of the end. Lot offers his two daughters instead, and then the angels have to save Lot from being seized, and they defeat the Sodomites' attempt to break into the house. Destruction is announced for the city, and Lot is advised to warn his sons-in-law who seem to be as stupid as he is. Finally the angels take Lot, his wife and daughters—this is a family of lingerers—and urge them to flee to the hills. Even at this breaking point Lot asks to go to a "small place" (the meaning of the name of the town, Zoar), and not to the hills. He is saved, but, as you remember, his wife looked back! The story of this family has yet another ugly chapter: Lot's drunkenness and the birth of the future Moab and Ammon from him and his daughters.

Q. 15. How is one to understand Abraham's dinner with the three mysterious guests?

It is simply a great story. One should read carefully the description of Abraham as the generous and gracious host, anticipating their needs, ordering up choice food and finally serving and waiting upon them in the shade of a tree. One of them is identified as *yhwh* (v. 1), and his role is to deliver the message to Sarah that she is to bear a son "this time next year." Another laughing episode! Eavesdropping, Sarah frankly laughs at the preposterous idea. Thus far there is someone always laughing when Isaac's name is brought up (Abraham in 17:17). That's one way of telling the story. Isaac's name means "(God) laughs" (cf. 21:6). Sarah's attempt to deny it and the insistence of *yhwh* is a master stroke in the narrative. The dinner is over and Abraham accompanies them on the way. As it turns out, the two subordinates have a mission to perform in

Sodom, and this provides the occasion for a strikingly intimate conversation between the Lord and Abraham (18:17–33).

"Shall I conceal from Abraham what I am about to do?" This remarkable question and soliloquy of the Lord demonstrates both the stature of Abraham and the task that he has to perform—to show his posterity they should follow the Lord "in righteousness and justice." Righteousness! Almost as if reading the mind of God, Abraham takes up this issue when the Lord is seeking to determine the moral situation of Sodom and Gomorrah (a task that is given to the other two guests). The famous bargaining of Abraham and the Lord begins, and the issue is the righteousness of God's action. "Will you indeed sweep away the righteous with the wicked?" Presupposed in this dialogue is the power of the innocent. Their presence, it is assumed, can save the wicked—it is better that God would let off the wicked than harm the innocent. This sense of individual and collective responsibility seems strange to us. But the power of the righteous to save the community is upheld by Abraham, and also acknowledged by the Lord. As the conversation continues, the requisite number of the righteous is pressed by Abraham and it descends from fifty to ten. "Shall not the judge of all the earth act justly?" The end of the conversation is phrased almost mysteriously in v. 33. It is the Lord who somewhat abruptly leaves. The issue has come down to ten just people, and Abraham is not given another opportunity to speak. However, there is a kind of sequel to it all. After two cities of the plain are destroyed, we read in 19:27–28 that Abraham returned early in the morning to the very place of the conversation and he looked out upon the plain, only to see the smoke ascending! He should have pressed for less than ten! The episode is not only remarkable for its vividness and the boldness of Abraham; it underscores a central problem of biblical thought: the justice of God. On the individual level the theme appears in its most anguished form in the book of Job and in many psalms. On the collective level it is taken up by the prophet Habakkuk and others (see Ez 14:12–20, and ponder the Deuteronomic view of God's action in history). It remains a mystery.

Q. 16. Who are the "three men" who dined in Abraham's dwelling?

I can give you the correct answer to that but it will not take away the mystery of their identity. In chapter 18 "they," in the plural, speak to him, until v. 13 when the Lord is explicitly introduced as catching out Sarah when she laughs at the divine announcement that she will be pregnant within the year. The "men" take their departure, two of them directly for Sodom, while the Lord has the long conversation with Abraham. The men are called "angels" (*mal'akim*) in 19:1 when they arrive in Sodom, but they are referred to as "men" until v. 15 when they are termed "angels." This is surely a confusing shift. What can be said with a fair amount of certainty? We have already mentioned (Q. 8 above) the existence of the heavenly court, "the sons of God," as they are usually called. They serve as counselors to the Lord, and apparently as an army if they are the "hosts" in the phrase, "Lord of Hosts."

When these heavenly beings are assigned to certain functions, they are frequently called "angels" (Greek *aggelos*, messenger). This usage is frequent enough in the Bible. A problem arises, especially in the Pentateuch, when the "angel of the Lord" seems to be identified with the Lord. Thus in Genesis 16, Hagar is speaking with a messenger of the Lord, but as the conversation develops, he is clearly identified with the Lord (16:10, and 16:13, "she called the Lord who spoke to her..."). This puzzling change in identity occurs several times: Hagar and her son (Gen 21:17–18), after the near sacrifice of Isaac (Gen 22:11–12, 15–18), when the Lord appears to Moses at the burning bush (Ex 3:2–3). One should note especially the appearance of a *mal'ak* in the Exodus narratives (especially Ex 23:20–22, "My Name is in him," i.e., in the messenger).

No satisfactory explanation for this switching of identity has been reached. It has been "explained" in various ways, e.g., that it is a later addition or interpolation that preserves the exalted character of the Lord who cannot be seen, or that there is a connection between the one who sends and the one who is sent, etc. In *ABD* 1, 248–53 C. A. Newsom has a succinct treatment of angels in the Old Testament, and with regard to the changing of identity she thinks that the "most likely" explanation is that this is a deliberate ambiguity which expresses a tension or paradox: the Lord is present and active, but no human being can have a direct encounter with God. This is not unlike the traditional view that the usage aims to preserve the exalted character of the Lord.

Q. 17. What incident do you consider to be the most important in the story of Abraham?

This is not an easy question to answer. Important might be the most appropriate word for the initial promises to Abraham (Gen 12:1–3), or for the covenants described in chapters 15 and 17. What is related there affects us all as the children of Abraham. But notice how everything seems to revolve around the idea of offspring. For this reason I personally find the *akedah*, or "binding" of Isaac, the most touching, and, as well, the most important. The *difference* in terminology is deliberate. Our Jewish brothers and sisters speak of the binding, and Christians speak of the sacrifice, of Isaac. In order to put chapter 22 in its proper perspective we have to recall some of the points that have been related above. First there is the totally improbable promise given to Abraham that he is to be the father of a great nation—despite the fact that he and Sarah are well beyond the age for having a family. Second, the promise is continually renewed, so much so that one begins to wonder what sense it makes. Abraham reminds the Lord on one occasion that things look so bleak that his servant Eliezer should be considered (15:2–3). But no, the Lord has his own plan. Third, when Ishmael is born of Hagar, thanks to the comfortable polygamy of that ancient culture, Abraham proposes Ishmael—in direct response to one of the Lord's frequent promises (17:18). He is trying his best to help the Lord out of the fix that he has created for himself. Nothing comes of it—until finally Isaac, the child of promise, appears (with appropriate laughter). Now those words of 22:1–2 lead to the climax. After all this trouble, after the repeated announcements of a child from Abraham's loins, and the promise of a future nation, God puts Abraham to a "test." In words that drip with a certain tenderness and with high emotional charge, Abraham is to take his son, his only one, whom he loves, and offer him up as a burnt offering! What sense does this make? The scene is memorable as Abraham starts the journey with servants and victim. The silence in the narrative is broken by Abraham's orders to the servant as they near the designated place. It is interesting that the boy carries the wood, but, as if to keep the lad from harm's way, Abraham carries the fire and the knife. The only question is the naive inquiry of Isaac. They have everything but the animal for sacrifice—where is it? "God will provide (literally, see).…" What kind of answer is that? Abraham knows the provision that God has already announced, but he leaves it as an open question. In a series of staccato verbs (22:9), Abraham makes all the arrangements and takes the knife to plunge it into his son—and he is stopped by the voice of the angel of *yhwh*.

Let us ponder the scene that has been unfolded before us. It is well known that child sacrifice was practiced fairly widely in the ancient world, and that it was viewed as a religious act. Perhaps at some point in the handing down of this story, it was aimed at prohibiting such an action. In such a case, the paternal instinct of Abraham would not be a primary issue; this was a proper religious rite (however, the tender accents of v. 2 suggest deep feeling in Abraham). The heart of the matter is Abraham's ability to allow God to go back on a promise as the sacrifice of Isaac seemed to imply. Offspring, nation, promises and covenants. What did all those things mean now? Many speak of Abraham's faith, of his obedience, and so forth, but such religious terminology—however correct—fails to capture the naked realism of his encounter with God in the land of Moriah. The observation of the author of the letter to the Hebrews is frankly rather flat; he seems to interpret Abraham from his own post-Resurrection belief: "He reasoned that God was able to raise even from the dead, and he received Isaac back as a symbol" (Heb 11:19, *NAB*). This typological interpretation was doubtless important for his audience, but it is at the expense of the "test" that is at the heart of the story. The exclamation of Abraham in v. 8 is picked up in the etiological explanation of the name of the place, *yhwh yir'eh* ("the Lord will see/provide"). But the reader feels that this is more than etiology; it is the happy cry of our father Abraham!

The most devastating comment (not commentary!) on the passage that I know of is that of the "melancholy Dane," Søren Kierkegaard. In the first part of his *Fear and Trembling* he reflects on Genesis 22 as he prepares to discuss the "teleological suspension of the ethical," i.e., what is one to do when one is commanded by God to perform such an act as this? He imagines various ways in which the story might end, and these serve to point up the excruciating nature of the situation. The first scenario is this: Abraham goes through all the motions, raises his knife—and Isaac cries out to the Lord for help. Good, Abraham says to himself, the boy thinks that it is I, not God, who want him slain. The second scenario: Abraham goes through all the preparations, and as he raises the knife to plunge it into the boy, he cannot do it, and simply lets the knife fall…and from that day forward Isaac never again spoke to his father!

Q. 18. Why is so little said about Isaac in the patriarchal history?

I really don't know. Your question is based on the fact that the only substantial treatment of Isaac is given in chapter 26, and the events described here seem to be variants of Abrahamic traditions. Thus the wife/sister theme is played out in 26:1–16 with King Abimelèch of the Philistines (an anachronism for this period) at Gerar. The episode of the water wells in 26:17–33 owes something to 21:22–34. Nonetheless, there are two charming stories that are associated with him, even if they deal primarily with someone else: the wooing of his wife (chapter 24, the longest chapter in the book), and the conflict of his two sons, Jacob and Esau.

The story of the marriage is important because the divine promises are to be continued through the line of Abraham. Hence Abraham commissions his (unnamed) servant to bring back "from my country" a wife for Isaac. Under no condition is Isaac to marry a Canaanite or fail to return. After a solemn gesture sealing his oath the servant departs. The scene immediately shifts to a well in the city of Nahor in Aram-naharaim. The servant's touching prayer in 24:12–14 for a providential sign whereby he may recognize the "right" woman for Isaac is verified by the actions of Rebekah in vv. 15–22. His gifts to her catch the attention of her brother Laban, and from that point on success is assured, but not without the servant rehearsing the whole story. Permission for the marriage is given, and the next memorable scene is between Isaac and Rebekah, who draws her veil when she is told that her future husband is walking over the field to meet her, "and he loved her" (24:64).

In contrast to this idyllic piece stands the complicated skein of stories of their descendants, Esau and Jacob. It is a series of conflicts. This begins in the very womb of Rebekah when her barrenness is answered by the clash of the unborn "twins" who are interpreted as two peoples, and the elder will serve the younger (contrary to the rights of primogeniture). Jacob is born after Esau, but gripping his heel! (an etiological explanation of the Hebrew name, Ya'aqob). The contrast between the two sons splits the affection of the parents as well. A harbinger of future developments lies in the famous story of Esau selling his birthright (*bekorah*, a play on *berakah* or blessing, which becomes the theme of chapter 27) for a mess of pottage. The blessing given by the blind Isaac illustrates the division between father and mother and also the children. Isaac has every intention of blessing the older boy, as proper custom demanded. Esau departs to bring home some game for his father to eat in order to bestow the blessing. The well-known transformation of Jacob into the "hairy" Esau by means of animal skin is achieved by the wily Rebekah, although there are tense moments as Isaac marvels that "Esau" has returned so quickly, but his touch reassures him: "the voice is the voice of Jacob, but the hands are those of Esau." Thus Jacob steals the blessing. The pathos of Esau's cry (27:34, 38) when he returns and finds there is no blessing left for him (the blessing cannot be revoked) is unmistakable. Isaac can only pronounce what amounts to an oracle presaging the relation between the two brothers and their descendants. Rebekah is again at work and succeeds in having Jacob sent to her brother's house to choose a wife—in contrast to Esau who marries an Ishmaelite (27:41–28:9). This is an excuse to deliver Jacob from Esau's murderous threat. We moderns cannot but be mystified at the various developments in this story. For example, why is a blessing simply unrepeatable? Because that's the way it was in the culture. And the final words of Isaac to Esau cannot be a blessing; Esau will serve his brother although ultimately he will achieve freedom (a comment on the future relations between Edom [Esau] and Israel). Moreover, one would think that the selection of the patriarchs should not involve the deceit and lies that are manifested in chapter 27. But there lies a significant point. The divine choice does not depend upon human goodness.

Q. 19. Did Abraham and the other patriarchs (and matriarchs) really exist?

We have already noted the shadowy existence of Isaac and the frequency with which doublets occur within the recorded lives of these people. Certainly these chapters do not constitute history as a modern person would understand the term. The relationship between the three patriarchs, Abraham, Isaac and Jacob, is described as genealogical: father, son and grandson. Yet the freedom with which these traditions have been woven together makes one wonder if this is not an oversimplification of what may have been a complicated historical process. Genealogies in the Bible are used for more than physical descent; they indicate relationships of various kinds (geographical, commercial, etc.). It is possible that we have an amalgam of traditions of the various later tribes of Israel. This can be exemplified in such traditions as those of Jacob and Esau that seem to mirror the later rivalry between Israel and Edom. Similarly, the incestuous birth (Gen 19:30–38) of Moab and Benammi (Ammon) are tales that reflect later geographical and historical animosities. One might best conclude that we are dealing with types of literature that do not afford us the means of answering the problem of historicity. What is undeniable is the firm belief that later Israel had in the divine guidance of its ancestors who lived under a promise that was in the process of fulfillment in Israel's history.

As for the matriarchs, the whole biblical culture leads us to expect a minimum of information concerning them, despite their importance. The reason, of course, is the patriarchal culture into which divine revelation was inserted. The role of women was not publicly appreciated, and they were for the most part (there are a few exceptions) relegated to familial functions. Looking back to Sarah and to Hagar, wives of Abraham, to Rebekah, and to Rachel and Leah, wives of Jacob, we realize that little attention is paid to them outside of functions of wife and mother. However, more and more attention is being given to them by feminist scholars (e.g., Phyllis Trible, *God and the Rhetoric of Sexuality* [Philadelphia: Fortress, 1978]). The patriarchalism of the Bible cannot be denied; it must be recognized as a fact, a limitation (however inevitable) of the biblical world and word. This is not the place to confront head-on the problem of inclusive and exclusive language in the Bible and in classical literature generally. We today are prisoners of the English language that has shaped us, and it is patriarchal. Until the language undergoes a change (necessarily a long period), only relatively minor, and hence unsatisfactory, modifications can be made in the direction of inclusive language. Such an effort was made in the 1991 revision of the psalms in the New American Bible—but much more remains to be done, despite the Roman congregation decisions of 1994 that were communicated to the United States.

Q. 20. Why are so many chapters given to the story of Jacob?

Perhaps the simplest answer is that more tales about his various adventures were handed down. But there is an important reason to consider: Jacob was held to be the immediate father of the twelve tribes of Israel. Directly or indirectly his life span extends from his remarkable birth in Genesis 25:26, gripping the heel of his brother Esau, down to his placid death in Egypt as described in Genesis 49:33, "when he drew up his feet into the bed, breathed his last, and was gathered to his people." But his final charge is that the sons shall bury him with his ancestors in Machpelah in the field that Abraham originally bought (Gen 23). Another reason can be drawn from the mysterious encounter with a "man" as described in Genesis 32:24–32. Jacob is returning to Canaan after his adventurous service with his cousin Laban and the marriage to both Leah and Rachel. When he is alone, about to cross the Jabbok and join his retinue, he wrestles all night with a man who finally dislocates his hip. But Jacob will not give up, and when the "man" requests, "Let me go because it is daybreak" (why could he not stay beyond sunrise?), Jacob refuses until he receives a blessing. At this point the "man" changes Jacob's name to Israel—a fundamental omen for the future (*nomen est omen*). A very puzzling scene. The reader may ask: Who won this match? Jacob is injured but the victor has to plead to be let go. It seems that the refusal to identify himself to Jacob makes the latter realize that he has been wrestling with a supernal being, even God: "I have seen God face to face, but even so I have been spared." That is why he called the place Peniel (face of God), and was filled with marvel because the accepted view was that if one saw God, death would ensue. The change of the name from Jacob to Israel is appropriately interpreted, "You have striven with God" and men, and have prevailed.

The figure of Jacob must have intrigued his descendants. The description of Esau indicates that the wily character of Jacob was to be preferred to the gruff personality of Esau. Moreover, there were signs of divine approval: the wrestling with the heavenly being, the visions at Bethel (Gen 28:10–22; 35:9–15). A vivid realism characterizes the description of Jacob's experience with his cousin Laban. He agrees to seven years of labor for the privilege of marrying Rachel, and Laban tricks him by giving him Leah instead. So Jacob, the "heel-gripper," gets a tidy comeuppance for the deceit practiced upon his own brother; the

younger (Rachel) will not go ahead of the firstborn (Leah), as Jacob suc-
ceeded in doing with Esau. But Jacob's love for Rachel was so great that
he served seven more years for her (Gen 29:30), verifying the earlier
statement of the author: Jacob served Laban seven years in order to gain
Rachel's hand, and these "seemed to him but a few days because of the
love he had for her" (29:20). However, Jacob never loses his wiliness,
and he succeeds in departing from Laban with adequate riches (Gen
30:25–31:55). There is something very pathetic and endearing in
Jacob's response to the question of the Egyptian pharaoh, "How long
have you lived?" "One hundred and thirty years," he replies, and then
adds: "Few and hard have been the years of my life" (Gen 47:9). Jacob
places Joseph under oath to bury him with their ancestors in Machpelah
(Gen 47:28–31; 49:29–33).

Q. 21. What is the episode of Judah and Tamar doing within the Joseph story?

That is not an easy question to answer, but I am glad that it was preserved and incorporated somewhere. It has little bearing on the Joseph
narrative, although Judah figures in it. In itself it is a neatly told story. The
situation for the heavy action in 38:12 is set up by the separation of Judah
from his brothers and his dealing with Canaanites. He marries a Canaanite
woman, and his first-born, Er, also marries a Canaanite, Tamar (meaning
"palm"). No reason is given for the Lord's "anger" against Er. His early
death was enough to suggest to anyone some kind of divine displeasure.
The ancients thought in a "post hoc, propter hoc" manner: if something
evil happened, it could be blamed on wrongdoing (or even what had the
appearance of wrongdoing, as when Uzzah touched the ark in 2 Samuel
6:6–7). According to the law it would be Onan's duty to raise up seed in
his brother's name. However, he refuses this duty and wastes the seed
(what is wrong about his action is not "onanism," but his refusal to fulfill
his obligation as a brother-in-law). He, too, dies, and the author sees in this
another example of divine displeasure. Judah promises the third son,
Shelah, to Tamar, but he is not sincere about it. Meanwhile, Tamar returns
to her father's house, probably suspecting Judah's duplicity.

Judah becomes a widower and goes out to seek some sexual con-
solation. This is where Tamar takes over the action. It seems that she

poses as a harlot (a "holy one," literally, devoted to a god) for Ashera or some divinity. She is not a "woman of the street," as we might judge from her actions but she deliberately has intercourse with Judah who does not recognize her. For payment she exacts a pledge by asking for his seal (a kind of I.D. for official identification) and staff. When their business is transacted, Tamar returns home to put on the garments of her widowhood. Later, Judah sends an animal in payment, but when Tamar cannot be located, he lets the matter drop. When he is notified a few months later that Tamar is with child as a result of harlotry, he is ready to condemn her to death. At this point she produces the pledge as the identity of the person who has impregnated her. The only decent thing that Judah does in the whole narrative is to admit she is "more righteous" than he is. Tamar then delivers twins, Perez and Zerah.

One reason why this story may have been preserved is that Perez figures in the line of David, according to Ruth 4:18–22. It is also worthy of note that Tamar appears in the genealogy of Jesus according to Matthew 1:3 and Luke 3:33. She is not the only woman to appear in Matthew; she is accompanied by Rahab (cf. Jos 2:1), Ruth, and the "wife of Uriah" (Bathsheba). In his commentary on Genesis in *HBC*, p. 115, J. Kselman points out the textual connections that the Judah story has with the rest of the Joseph narrative: "the failure to recognize a family member (38:15, 42:8); a deception involving a kid and a means of identification (37:31; 38:17–18); the words of Jacob's sons ('recognize this garment') in 37:32 paralleled by Tamar's ('recognize to whom these belong') in 38:23. And Judah's recognition of his seal and staff (v. 26) recalls Jacob's recognition of Joseph's garment (37:33)."

The episode is a good example of the Levirate law, although the law is not followed in this case. According to the law in Deuteronomy 25:5–10, it was a serious obligation to keep alive the name of the dead brother-in-law (levirate comes from the Latin name for brother-in-law, *levir*). Once again we are reminded of the patriarchal caste of Israelite society. There are also territorial concerns, as the episode of the daughters of Zelophehad exemplifies (Num 27:1–11). Zelophehad died during the wilderness period, leaving five daughters and no sons (hence, no male heir). The daughters bring the case before Moses who appeals to the Lord for a decision: Can the daughters inherit? The Lord decides in their favor, but they have to marry within their own tribe in order to prevent the inheritance from going outside of the tribe (cf. Num 36:6–7).

Q. 22. Would you characterize the Joseph narrative (Genesis 37–50) as a story within a story?

That is a good way of putting it, because the death of Joseph is reported in the chapter immediately following the description of Jacob's last words. Moreover the story of Joseph is quite different in style from the patriarchal narratives. It has been called a "novella," a kind of short story that deals with the adventures of brothers. Jacob figures in the narrative, but from a distance. Yet the author has adroitly worked in the memory of the father who is bereft of his favored son and does not want to lose any more. His memory is constantly evoked in the conversation between Joseph and his brothers (42:13, 38; 43:6, 14, 27–28) and it is a primary motif in Judah's plea (44:19–34). The dramatic potential of the story has been realized in the trilogy by the famous German writer, Thomas Mann (*Joseph and His Brothers,* 1933–44), and not too long ago there was a Broadway play on the theme of the multicolored coat of Joseph. Although the individual characters in the story are sharply etched, there is a tribal aura given to them, as in the case of Judah and in the detail given to the sons of Joseph who are born in Egypt: Manasseh and especially Ephraim. In the description of Jacob's blessing of Joseph's sons, the old man insists on blessing the younger, Ephraim (recall the episode of Jacob and Esau receiving Isaac's blessing in Genesis 27). Ephraim, of course, becomes the strongest tribe in the north; the future history of the nation is being anticipated, as it is also foreseen in the blessings that Jacob bestows upon his sons in chapter 49 (especially Judah, of whom it is said that the scepter shall not depart from him—a reference to the dominion exercised by David).

But the real story lies in the dramatic events surrounding the relationship of Joseph and his brothers. As the favorite of his father (he and Benjamin were born of Rachel the beloved), he is hated by his brothers, and it is only his capture by a passing tribe of Midianites that saves him from their murderous envy and brings him to Egypt. His spectacular gifts in dream interpretation ensure his rise in the pharaoh's court. Now the drama begins. The famine forces his brothers to go to Egypt for relief.

What follows reminds one of a cat and mouse game. Joseph knows well who they are and perhaps wonders if they have changed. They do not recognize him, and they have to suffer the indignities that he visits upon them: accusation of spying and imprisonment. They are finally freed (except for Simeon who remains as a hostage). They are sent back with the command not to return unless they bring the youngest son (Benjamin, the uterine brother of Joseph). Then they find that their money has been secretly returned to them! What a mysterious and arbitrary man, this Egyptian! Although old Jacob avows that they shall never go back with Benjamin, they do so. It must be admitted that the sudden somersaults in the story may point to a combination of sources, or at least the addition of supplements. One can compare the favorable characterization of Reuben in 42:22, 37 with the words of Judah in 44:32. Their second trip during another famine is also weird. Their offer to return the money that had been given them on the first trip is waved aside, and they are invited to dine with Joseph. Then they are served according to seniority! But another trick awaits them. Their return home is prevented by the accusation that Joseph's personal divining cup has been stolen by them. So sure of their integrity are they that they pledge death for the guilty one and slavery for all. Mischievously, this is refused; only the "guilty" one will be enslaved. And of course it is in Benjamin's sack that the cup is found. Now Judah gives his famous speech (Gen 44:18–34), an impassioned plea that stresses the grief that will kill their father—let Judah be imprisoned in place of Benjamin. This is the climactic point. When the would-be fratricides are ready to make sacrifices for each other, it is time for Joseph to reveal his identity. He does this in the moving passage in 45:1–15: "I am Joseph. Is my father still alive?" and he explains to the speechless brothers: "God sent me before you to preserve a remnant for you in the land. Not you but God sent me here…" (44:7–8). Later, he has to repeat this to his brothers who never seem able to be at ease with him: "You intended harm for me, but God intended it for good" (50:20).

The Joseph story has been characterized as a specimen of Old Testament "wisdom" writing; it supposedly exemplifies the rise of a courtier and his fortune, if he is wise (as Joseph was). But this interpretation, originally proposed by G. von Rad, has not caught on. Rather, it is a story of divine providence that has been intertwined with the Jacob narrative and used to indicate how the descendants of Abraham, to whom the land of Canaan was promised, ended up in Egypt. This is the preparation for the adventures related in the book of Exodus.

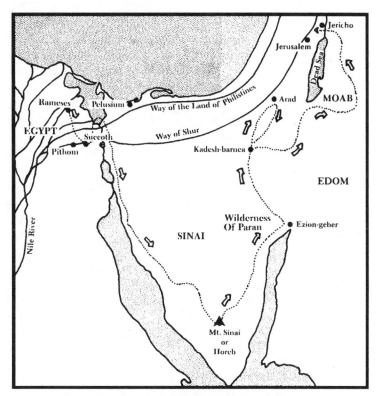

The Traditional Exodus Escape Route

EXODUS/SHEMOTH

Q. 23. The book of Exodus is about much more than an escape. Is the name "Exodus" or even the Hebrew word "Shemoth" the best name for this book?

I would say no, they are not, but one should recall there is a rationale for both names. As we saw, the Hebrew names for the five books are derived from the opening words (like a papal encyclical). Here

Shemoth or "Names" refers to Jacob's sons, and the stage is set for the experience of his descendants in Egypt, "the tribes of Israel." What has thus far been family stories (in Genesis: Abraham, Isaac and Jacob) now will be the experience of the "children of Israel" (Ex 1:1). The Greek tradition of the name Exodus underlines the dramatic saving events of chapters 1–18, but that leaves the Sinai events unmentioned, and the Sinai story continues into chapter 10 of the book of Numbers, when Israel departs from Sinai. The exodus experience itself became so central to Israel's self-understanding, so deeply impressed in its memory, that one hardly adverts to the fact than only a few key chapters describe the actual exit. The surrounding events merge with the liberation from Egypt. The story of the midwives, the call of Moses, the forced labor, the contest of Moses and Aaron (or better, the Lord) with the pharaoh which culminates in the final plague that propels the people out of Egypt—all this is conjured up by the mere mention of the word "exodus." And this is only half the story. Guidance through the desert, the covenant with the Lord at Sinai, the construction of the desert tabernacle, all fill out the desert experience of the motley crew (so termed in 12:38 when they begin their journey). The refugees arrive at Sinai in Exodus 19:1 where they remain until Numbers 10:11, a period of about one year. Only in the book of Numbers do they undertake the last leg of the journey to Canaan—and then only to languish for forty years in the desert. Even in Deuteronomy they are left on the brink, as it were, poised to enter, but remaining in the plains of Moab.

Q. 24. Are there any references in Egyptian records to the existence of Joseph or to Moses and the exodus?

No, there are no such references. The book itself refers to the change in the fortunes of the people: "a new king arose, who knew not Joseph" (Ex 1:8), and many conjectures have been made about the historical meaning behind this, but there is nothing really certain. One may perhaps infer that a native Egyptian line came into power, and naturally took advantage to create a labor force from the strangers in their midst. There are only two historical details that have a bearing—and it is remote—on the biblical text. The first is the mention of the cities of Pithom and Rameses (1:11) where the Israelites were forced to labor;

there may be some association here with the Egyptian pharaoh, Rameses II (about 1290-1224). The second is the so-called stele of Merneptah, the son of Rameses II, which refers to a people in Canaan, Israel, that it claims to have been devastated. The thirteenth century is the date accepted by many scholars for the exodus and entry into Canaan, but it must be admitted that the evidence is thin.

Q. 25. Are there not two versions (doublets) concerning the call of Moses?

Yes, such a conclusion seems inescapable. A careful comparison between Exodus 3:1–4:17 and 6:2–7:7 (usually ascribed to J and to P) is instructive; we learn from these different accents the way in which Israel could develop central traditions without feeling compelled to choose between them. The J narrative begins with the famous episode of the burning bush "at Horeb, the mountain of God" (apparently Sinai is meant)—burning, but without being consumed. The Lord identifies himself with the God of Abraham, Isaac and Jacob, and Moses immediately reacts by hiding his face lest he see God and die. The Lord has heard the cry of the people and is about to commission Moses to lead them out of Egypt. But Moses is unwilling: "Who am I...?" is his reply. Indeed, to every point that the Lord raises, Moses has objections: When the people ask me your name, what shall I say? Suppose they don't believe me? I am a very poor speaker—send someone else! If this is an implicit plea to send Aaron, the Lord will have none of it. He knows well that Aaron is eloquent, but the arrangement will be this: he will speak to the people but Moses will be a representative of God to a prophet, putting the divine words in Aaron's mouth (Ex 4:14–16, 30).

The second account is less dramatic, and more wordy. Yet the objection of Moses is expressed again (6:30), and the analogy appears again. The Lord tells Moses that he is to be like God to the pharaoh, and Aaron will be his prophet. The commission itself does not have the drama of the theophany at the burning bush. However it states the essentials: Israel is to be told of their coming deliverance, and the familiar priestly formula is used to express that they shall be the Lord's people and he shall be their God (6:7). The promises to Abraham, Isaac and Jacob are to be fulfilled.

Q. 26. What is the meaning of the name *yhwh* that the Lord reveals to Moses (Ex 3:13–15)?

That is a very difficult question. First of all, one might ask if it is a refusal to reveal the name. What sense does "I am who I am" or "I will be whatever I will be" make? One should recall the significance of the name in the Old Testament—it stands for the person, and a knowledge of the name was sometimes regarded as a means of wielding power over the other (cf. Gen 32:30 where the superhuman "wrestler" refuses to divulge his name to Jacob, at the same time that he changes Jacob's name to Israel). In the context of Exodus 3, however, many regard the meaning of the name as an assurance: I AM with you to deliver you (cf. vv. 13, 16). In 3:14 the Lord gives the name in the first person: "Thus shall you tell the Israelites, 'I AM has sent me to you.'" Finally, in v. 15 the name is put in the third person, *yhwh*. God says: "Tell the Israelites, *yhwh*, the God of your ancestors...has sent me to you.'" From an etymological point of view it has been argued that *yhwh* refers to God as Creator, the one who causes to be. But this is quite uncertain.

The mystery that attaches to the sacred name revealed here has never disappeared. Out of reverence for the name, the Israelites early on substituted the term Adonai ("milord," or "my master"). Later, *hashem* (the name) also came to be used. The probable vocalization of the sacred name is *yahweh*, and this has recently become popular among Christians—a development that goes against the traditional rendering of the name as Kyrios (Greek form), Dominus (Latin), and LORD (in small caps) in English. In any case, Jehovah is a linguistic atrocity. It illegitimately combines the vowels that suggest Adonai to the reader with consonants of the sacred name (j and y sound the same in many languages). This issue of the sacred name is no light matter and the Jewish *reverence* for the mystery of God and the name could well be imitated by Christians.

There is a striking scene on Mount Sinai that reveals the significance of the sacred name. After the smashing of the original tablets of the Decalogue, Moses cuts two stone tablets and ascends Mount Sinai alone. Then, "having come down in a cloud, the Lord stood with him there and proclaimed his name, 'Lord.' Thus the Lord passed before him and cried out, 'The Lord, the Lord, a merciful and gracious God, slow to anger and rich in kindness and fidelity, continuing his kindness for a thousand generations, and forgiving wickedness and crime and sin...'"

(Ex 34:5–7, *NAB*). Here the Lord ceremoniously proclaims the name and associates with it the marvelous mercy that Israel never forgot. These characteristics of the Lord are echoed throughout the rest of the Old Testament: Num 14:18; Dt 5:9–10; Pss 86:15, 103:8; 145:8; Jon 4:2, etc. The short form, -jah (or -iah/-yah) appears many times, especially in proper names like Isaiah or Jeremiah.

Q. 27. How is one to understand the ten plagues of Egypt?

These are described in Exodus 7:14–12:32, and they are not easy to understand because of the artificial character of the events. The narrative is not describing what happened according to historical rules. Evidence for this comes from the fact that it is composed of events from the different traditions, J and P, to make up the series. Both J and P have seven plagues, and these are woven together to yield nine. Psalm 105, a clear parallel reference, has only eight, so there must have been a rather loose understanding of the events themselves. Later on, in the book of the Wisdom of Solomon written near to the time of Christ, there is even more freedom in dealing with these events. The nature of the narrative is dramatic: Will the Lord's plan for Israel's deliverance prevail over the pharaoh's power? The reader is invited to an inner view of the struggle: at times the pharaoh will be obstinate of his own will; at other times the Lord will "harden" the pharaoh's heart. But with all the drama there is never any question about the eventual victor. The tension of the story is heightened by the ability of the Egyptian magicians to duplicate some of the plagues. (For example, the Nile was turned into blood. Where did the magicians get the water to duplicate this feat? The writer does not bother about such details.) Of course, the magicians eventually fail (Ex 8:18). This is not a series of "miracle" stories. Miracle is the wrong word to use of these events if it is understood as a suspension of a law of nature. The Hebrews would not have understood what that means. Everything that happens is the Lord's doing, the usual and the unusual, because nothing escapes divine sovereignty. For them, these were "signs" and "marvels" that achieved victory over an unwilling and deceitful pharaoh. One should not "rationalize" on these events, as some have tried to do with the first plague, namely, that it represented the annual overflow of the Nile which drew into itself the reddish sediment of the sand through which it courses.

The tenth plague stands apart from the others (which are notably marked off in sets of three). It is associated with a liturgy, the Passover (Pesach, or Pasch). It was to be explained in tradition to children (Ex 12:27): "This is the Passover sacrifice to the Lord who passed over the houses of the Israelites in Egypt. He struck down the Egyptians but spared our houses." Before the plague itself is described, the liturgy and meaning are given according to the priestly source. It seems to be connected with the sacrifice of an animal in the springtime to secure the good of the flock. This also became associated with the feast of Unleavened Bread. Originally this marked a new turn, a new beginning. The bread was now eaten without the leaven from the previous year, and for the first seven days of the barley harvest only the bread made from the new grain was allowed. The two feasts were associated in Israelite tradition; originally they were simply customary practices of a peasant people, but now they were invested with historical significance, the escape from destruction in Egypt.

Q. 28. Is the Red Sea the same as the Reed Sea?

No, they are really quite different. The Red Sea is a rather large body of water that separates Africa from the Arabian peninsula. It narrows to the north into what is called the Gulf of Suez. We owe the identification of the "sea" crossed by the Israelites as the Red Sea to the Septuagint translation. This is the way it translated *yam suph* (10:18; 13:18). But this late (circa 200 B.C.) identification cannot be correct. The literal translation of the Hebrew terms would be "sea of Reeds," and this doubtless refers to the marshy lands that connect northern Egypt with the Sinai peninsula. Others understand the Hebrew term to mean the "sea of the End (Extinction)." This would be taken as an allusion to the Lord's conquest of chaos and Sea as mythological expression of the victory over the pharaoh and the deliverance from captivity. There are too many geographical uncertainties for us to be able to retrace the path taken by the Israelites from Egypt to the Sinai peninsula.

Q. 29. Are the Song of the Sea, the Song of Moses, and the Song of Miriam all one and the same?

The first term indicates the poem in Exodus 15:1–18 by its content; the second indicates the same poem by its presumed author, Moses; the third indicates the song attributed to Miriam in Exodus 15:21, which is one verse, and the same as the opening verse of the Song in 15:1. This verse could be a refrain intoned by Miriam, but some would argue that the entire Song in Exodus 15:1–18 is hers (there are many examples of triumphant war songs by women in the Old Testament). The Song itself gives still another description of the crossing at the sea by the Israelites. You will recall (Ex 14:21–31) that the actual crossing is described as a victory wrought by the Lord while the Israelites simply witness the event. The Israelites are caught between the Egyptians and the water. But overnight God dries the bed of the sea with a strong east wind. The Israelites cross over, but the waters catch the Egyptians in their pursuit—all this the work of the Lord. According to the priestly source, Moses stretches out his hand at the bidding of the Lord and splits the waters. The Israelites walk through the sea which forms a wall of water on both sides. The pursuing Egyptian army perishes when the water rushes over them. In the hymn of Exodus 15 there is some humor in the way that the Lord is described as tossing or throwing Egyptians into the sea (horse and rider, although the earlier text mentioned only chariot and charioteer). There seems to be an allusion to the well-known Canaanite myth of the battle with *Yam*, or Sea (vv. 4–5, 8, 10, 12). The cry in v. 12 celebrates the incomparability of the Lord. No other god can equal the Lord. Once again we are reminded of the fact that monotheism in Israel was a doctrine that only slowly matured. At this point there is no denial of other gods. They exist, but they simply cannot be viewed on the same level as the Lord; this is a kind of henotheism.

That the Song is a later composition is clear from what follows. It began with the escape from the Egyptians, who were eventually "swallowed into the earth" (i.e., the depths of Sheol), and the perspective now changes to the occupation of Canaan. All of Israel's enemies seem to be immobilized before the advance of what must have been a rag-tag army (vv. 14–16; the mention of Philistia suggests a later date, perhaps the eleventh century, for the composition of the Song). The progress continues, describing Israel's taking possession of the hills of Canaan (or possibly Zion itself—but this did not happen until the time of David). The exuberance of these lines overlooks the hard realities involved in the later descriptions of Israel trying to penetrate the land of Canaan (cf. Num 20–22).

Q. 30. Why did Israel's "murmuring in the desert" receive so much attention in the tradition?

That is not any easy question to answer. It is easier to understand the big issues, such as the episode of the golden calf and later on the refusal to follow Joshua and Caleb into Canaan. But the constant bickering, murmuring, and even revolt against Moses are a surprise. The treatment of Israel is milder in Exodus 15:22–17:16 than in Numbers 11:1–12:16; 16:1–17:12; 20:1–12 (Meribah); 25:1–16 (Baal of Peor). Perhaps one can say that the incredible honesty of Israel's writings is the outstanding characteristic of its recording of the traditions. Moses is constantly emphasizing fidelity and obedience in his speeches in Deuteronomy, but also threatening with death.

In connection with this perhaps the most mysterious question of all is Moses himself. Why did he not enter the Promised Land? This remained a puzzle for Israel, and several times the text returns to this unexpected fact. One can compare the following texts and yet fail to come up with a clear reason: Numbers 20:7–13; 27:14; Deuteronomy 1:37; 3:23–29; 32:51–52; Exodus 17:1–7. Perhaps the most common reason advanced is that Moses struck the rock twice to produce water— the second stroke being a sign of his doubts. This interpretation is entirely uncalled for, and is read into the text (contrast Exodus 17:1–7 with Numbers 20:7–13). Nor can one find an intelligible explanation in the phrase that Moses and Aaron were not faithful "in showing forth my holiness before the Israelites" (Num 20:12; Dt 32:51–52). One gets the impression that the Israelites were never able to understand this, and that they circled around the problem in the texts indicated above without being able to solve it. When we read the full and reverent description of Moses in Deuteronomy 34, itself suffused with a mysterious air, we get the impression that this was simply the way it was supposed to be—no questions asked. See Q. 55 for a fuller discussion in the light of the texts in Numbers and Deuteronomy.

Q. 31. How many covenants are made at Sinai?

I think your question concerns the covenant (Ex 19–24) and its renewal after the episode of the golden calf (Ex 32–34). Hence the short answer to your question is one covenant, and one renewal after it was broken. The Hebrew word *berith* means pact or agreement. This can exist among humans, but the important usage is religious: the covenant between the Lord and Israel, "You shall be my people and I shall be your God." In recent times comparisons have been made between this covenant and the suzerainty (as well as promissory) covenants that have been found in the ancient Near Eastern world, but many dispute the historical connections. The language of Exodus 19:4–6 is particularly lovely: "I bore you up on eagles' wings...you shall be my special possession....All the earth is mine; you shall be to me a priestly kingdom and a holy people." In an impressive ceremony of fire, smoke, and earthquake the covenant is announced, and the stipulations are pronounced: the Ten Commandments, and what is usually called the code of the covenant (Ex 20:22–23:33). The covenant is sealed in a lengthy ritual, with the sprinkling of the blood of the covenant upon the people. The event is followed (24:9–11) by a very unusual appearance of God to Moses and several others who partake of a sacred meal and also "see" God, but without dying!

The Ten Commandments are examples of apodictic law (you shall/you shall not—without any conditions attached). They are perhaps the best known part of the Bible, but not always for the best reasons. They stress fundamental values, indeed, but they have also been interpreted superficially as a kind of short-term measuring rod for moral conduct. Too many important aspects of moral action disappear under the broad universal negatives that make up the majority of the commands in the Decalogue. It is noteworthy that the new *Catechism of the Catholic Church* (1992) devotes over one hundred pages to breaking down the Commandments into specific areas. It is maybe debatable if this is the best pedagogical move, but it is supplemented in the *Catechism* by about one hundred pages dealing with the virtues and other aspects of the moral life. For discussion of the two forms of the Decalogue, see Q. 77.

The code of the covenant (Ex 20:22–23:33) is an example of mainly casuistic or conditional laws (if...then...). For example, "If someone opens a pit or digs a pit and leaves it uncovered and an ox or ass falls into it, the owner of the pit is to make restitution, giving the price to the owner, but keeping the dead animal" (21:33–34). A careful examination of this code indicates that it presupposes a sedentary society, and thus must date after the entry into Canaan. There is mention of slaves, fields, vineyards, etc.—in other words, a more advanced state of life than that experienced in a desert. It is not a code that is "revealed" by God and then "prophesied" by Moses as the way to live in Canaan. Rather, it grew up from the initial experience of the Israelites in their new land. Only then would there have been slavery (21:2–11) and care for aliens (23:9), and only then would farming have been taken for granted, as in chapter 23. Particularly worthy of note is the considerate treatment dealt out to the "resident alien," a stranger, even a non-Israelite, living among them; they are to be accorded protective rights. Israel should know, for they were once aliens in Egypt (see Q. 63). Perhaps the most famous "law" is the *lex talionis*, or talion law, usually phrased shortly as an "eye for an eye" (21:23–24). This law (already found in the celebrated Code of Hammurabi) is frequently misunderstood. Its purpose is to ensure equity in punishment, and to keep vengeance from going to excess, beyond what the wrongdoing merits. This was a necessary law where the communal sense of a group often led to extreme measures of revenge. In 23:1–9 are admirable social laws dealing with false witness, the possessions of one's enemy, care for the poor, bribery, etc.

Q. 32. Why are there two long descriptions about the production of the desert tabernacle?

Your question refers to Exodus 25–31, and 35–40, which are almost a verbatim rendition of each other. In the first Moses gives orders as to the execution of the work, and in the second the work is actually carried out. There is no certain answer to your question, but I would point out that the two blocks are separated by the remarkable chapters 32–34 that recount the episode of the golden calf, the smashing of the tablets of the Decalogue, and a renewal of the covenant. This makes for high drama in the midst of an otherwise prosaic description of temple furnishings. The description of the tabernacle is from the P tradition, which may have had the final say in the formation of the Torah. There has been much discussion whether the description is not a retrojection of the Solomonic Temple. However, one cannot discount the tradition that the Lord accompanied the refugees from Egypt, and tents for the divinity are known from ancient Ugarit. Be that as it may, it is important to have some perspective on the tabernacle, or tent. The main sanctuary consisted of a holy place that formed the entrance into the Most Holy Place where the Lord dwelt. Within the latter was the Ark of the Covenant, a relatively small box containing the two tablets of the law. On top of it was a golden plate where the invisible Lord was enthroned on the cherubim. One may indeed wonder if what was ostensibly a portable shrine could be at the same time so elaborate, along with the other accoutrements for worship such as the lampstand, the altar of incense, the sacrificial altar, etc.

More interesting and mysterious are chapters 32–34. The story line was broken by the legislation concerning the tabernacle while Moses was up on the mountain accepting the stone tablets, "written with the finger of God" (31:19). It resumes with the episode of the golden calf. This text is somewhat ambiguous; it seems to have an overlay from the famous "sin of Jeroboam" described in 2 Kings 12:26–29. In order to forestall a visit to Jerusalem Temple by any of the citizens of the northern kingdom of Israel, Jeroboam established shrines at Dan and Bethel, and installed "images" of bulls. These could be taken as thrones for the invisible Lord, but since the bull figured in the Baal cult, it became easier to confuse Yahweh and Baal, and a certain syncretism developed, in which one god's qualities are shared in describing another god. This worship was judged as idolatrous (e.g., Hos 4:12–19). Exodus 32:4b is repeated in 2 Kings 12:28: "This is your god/gods, O Israel, who brought you up from the land of Egypt." The word god (*'elohim*) can be translated in the singular or plural. If understood in the plural, it is clearly unorthodox. If it is understood in the singular, it is contrary to the command to construct an image. Notice that this "god" is acknowledged as the god of the exodus and Aaron builds an altar before it. Moses makes a brave attempt to intercede before the Lord for the people, but the Lord threatens to start over again and make of Moses a great people! There is a vivid scene in which Moses smashes the tablets, but again he intercedes for the people and it appears that they will not be wiped out.

Chapter 33 deals with the problem of divine presence. God will send an angel before them, more or less taking the place of the Lord. In Exodus 33:12–16 there is a face-off between God and Moses about the Lord leading the people. The dialogue is confusing because everything is so indirect. It ends with Moses' request to see the Lord's glory. The Lord concedes as much as possible: the divine goodness will pass by; the Lord will proclaim the sacred name, and also the divine favor and mercy (this does occur in Exodus 34:5–6). But that is all; Moses cannot live if he sees the face of the Lord. Instead, the Lord tells him that while he is in the cleft of a nearby rock, the divine hand will shield Moses as the Lord passes by. When the hand is withdrawn, "you will see my back, but my face is not to be seen" (Ex 33:23). This is surely one of the most startling scenes described in the Old Testament.

Chapter 34 has been interpreted in several ways. As it stands it seems to be a renewal of the covenant (34:10), and it has been conjectured that the various commands belong to the Yahwist version of the Decalogue, a kind of cultic or ritual decalogue. But this is quite speculative. As in chapter 33, there is an ending (34:29–30) that has become famous: "the horned Moses." The most striking representation of this is Michelangelo's magnificent sculpture in Rome—the one he is said to have struck on the knee and commanded to speak! This sculpture has Moses with horns, a rather unexpected association! But the Vulgate Latin Bible of Jerome, which was then the current Bible of Western Europe, so described Moses: with a *facies cornuta*, a horned face. This is a very literal translation of the Hebrew, which certainly has the term for "horn" (*qrn*), but it can also be rendered as "ray," hence "radiant," and this would seem to be the reason for the veil that Moses wore.

Q. 33. You passed over my question about the tabernacle. How can you have a tabernacle in the desert?

It all depends on the way you conceive of a tabernacle. The desert tabernacle, except for the veiled sanctuary, is really an open-air rectangular enclosure and the whole affair is portable. This means that the wooden frames and the precious cloths could be taken down and carried. What was this portable sanctuary or tabernacle proper? It is rather laborious to read chapters 25–40 of Exodus, which belong mainly to the priestly tradition, at least without also consulting some reference book that would provide a general picture. The desert tabernacle was also called "the tent of meeting," and there is a full description of how the Lord and Moses would meet there and confer under cover of a cloud, as the people, in front of their own tents, would bow low (Ex 33:7–11). Here oracles from the Lord would be received as the Lord talked to Moses "face to face." Sometimes this is placed within the Tabernacle proper, and sometimes without. The priestly tradition also used the word "dwelling" (*mishkan*), or tent that is pitched in some place. (Recall that in John 1:14 God is described as pitching a tent by the fact of the incarnation of the Logos.)

The desert tabernacle has been the object of considerable skepticism because it would seem to be cumbersome for a people on the move (taking down and putting up again), and the sources of the valuable materials that were used in it would not have been easily available in the desert. Moreover, the structure itself resembles closely the later Solomonic Temple. Hence opinions about it differ. But a general idea of the structure is necessary for the biblical reader. Let us start from the outside. There was a rectangular enclosure that formed a courtyard, where the altar for sacrifice and a large vessel for ablutions would have been located (Ex 30:17–21). The main edifice was the sanctuary itself: the Holy of Holies and the Holy Place (only a veil separating them). The Holy of Holies contained the Ark of the Covenant, with the cherubim (winged animals—so much for your chubby angelic figures of renaissance art) on which the invisible Lord was enthroned. The Holy Place housed the altar of incense, the seven-branched candlestick and the showbread (an offering of a dozen loaves of unleavened bread replaced every Sabbath). This sanctuary was covered over by precious veils and held up by wooden frames. The later history of the desert tabernacle is debated. It seems to have been at Shiloh (cf. Jos 18:1), and even to have been located within Solomon's Temple (cf. 1 Kgs 8:4; that is repeated in 2 Chr 5:5). But within the Pentateuch it is the scene of many happenings.

Q. 34. What did the Ark of the Covenant mean to the ancient Israelite?

It meant several things. It was only a small box of acacia wood (roughly 4 feet x 2 x 2; a cubit's length is hard to determine) and gold-plated. Thus, of itself it would seem to be less than imposing, although Exodus 37:1–6 describes its rings of gold for the gold-plated poles by which it was carried. It was used as a palladium, a war banner, as we learn from 1 Samuel 4–6, and its capture by the Philistines was looked upon as tragedy and crisis. Already in Numbers it seems to fulfill such a function. When the Israelites decamped, the Ark was carried in front, and Moses would say: "Arise, O Lord! May your enemies be scattered, and may your foes flee from your presence!" (Num 10:35).

The name differs in two traditions: in D it is the Ark of the Covenant (*berith*); and in P it is the Ark of Testimony (*'eduth*). The two terms mean practically the same thing (e.g., see the footnotes in the NRSV at Exodus 26:34). Perhaps the covenant for P was not to be associated with the Ark, since this was eventually lost or destroyed (by 587), but the covenant was eternal. In the Deuteronomic tradition the Ark is merely the place where the tablets of the law were deposited (cf. Deuteronomy 10:5, where the making of the Ark is attributed to Moses, not Bezalel; in Deuteronomy 31:26, the "book of the Law" is also deposited here, as a witness against Israel for the future). The Ark was also called the "footstool" of God (1 Chr 28:2; cf. also Pss 99:5; 132:7). Thus it would seem that the invisible Lord was enthroned upon the cherubim (1 Sam 4:4) with the Ark as the footstool. The Ark has many adventures in the historical books, and it was a stroke of genius on David's part to settle the Ark in Jerusalem.

LEVITICUS/WAYYIQRA'

Q. 35. Would you explain the names given to the third book of the Torah?

As with all the other Hebrew titles for the books of the Torah, the title is the first word, "and he called"—*wayyiqra'*. The reference is to the Lord's summoning Moses to communicate laws about the liturgy. The English title comes from the Latin and Greek tradition that more or less identified levites and priests. But neither title is really satisfactory. Early in rabbinic tradition the book was called the "Law of the Priests," which is far more adequate. But because deuteronomic theology spoke of "the levitical priests" (e.g., Dt 17:9), it appears that at some point priests and levites were identified, although this was not to last.

Leviticus is perhaps the book least read by Christians, but it is far more interesting than it appears to be at first sight. It is helpful to distinguish two main sections: 1–16 and 17–27. While the whole is the work of the priestly writers, the first part deals especially with various rituals, and the second part has been called the "Holiness Code," because of its strong emphasis on holiness (e.g., 19:2, "You shall be holy for I the Lord your God am holy"). While the work contains much ancient material (it should be recalled that this work is inserted into the Sinai context, and that the P tradition constitutes most of the text from Exodus 19 to Numbers 10), it received its final form after the exile. It lays down the doctrine of holiness (see Q. 40) to guide the post-exilic community, and is interpreted as God-given law. Over thirty times in the book, one reads: "The Lord said to Moses…."

Q. 36. Since there exists no temple now for priests to officiate in, what value has the book of Leviticus?

Your questions sounds as if the work was merely an antiquarian document and has no value for the modern Christian, or even the modern Jew, for that matter. But this is a short-sighted view. There are several values in this work that just off-hand I would enumerate: (1) the reverence for the Lord as displayed in the cultic laws; (2) a fuller understanding of divine holiness especially as this is reflected in Leviticus 18 (part of the so-called "holiness code," as chapters 17–26 are called); (3) the meaning of sacrifice. One could go on and on, and I am sure that a careful reading would reveal even deeper significance. But your question is particularly important because it raises a matter of principle, namely, we may not dismiss lightly any part of the Bible on the basis of relevance, or personal preferences. I am not denying that we all have preferences—favorite chapters or books to which we often return. But the point is that we should not simply neglect certain parts for merely personal and perhaps superficial reasons. One of the key elements of the liturgical reform of Vatican Council II was to make available large stretches of the Bible that perhaps many Catholics had never before read or had heard read in the liturgy. The threefold cycle in the Sunday readings, and the twofold cycle of the first reading for the weekdays, is a vast improvement. But even then, the choices might have been better (I may be showing my own bias and preferences now). For example, the wisdom books of the Old Testament open many windows on experiential realities, but the forty-two chapters of Job are represented by only eight readings; the eight chapters of the Song of Songs have only one reading, with a choice given among the alternatives in the wedding ceremony, and on December 21. The exception by far is Sirach: fifty-one chapters and twenty-five readings (some repeated, e.g., the famous chapter 24). And Leviticus? There are five readings for the twenty-seven chapters. So improvements could be made by a better distribution among the books and an improved choice of texts. However, it is difficult to avoid partiality in this matter. Perhaps new cycles could be created for optional or even mandatory alternative use. The lectionary proposed after the Council (and adopted and modified by many of the mainline Protestant churches) is certainly not written in stone.

Q. 37. What relationship do the levites and the priests have to one another?

This is a very complicated question; the short answer would be that the levites eventually become a kind of lesser clergy in the service of the Temple—at least in the post-exilic period. The early history is not easy to unravel. According to Genesis, Levi was born to Jacob by Leah. The history of the descendants is complicated. Moses is of levitical descent (Ex 2:1), and during the desert period the levites are portrayed as carrying out cultic functions. The tribe came to be set apart as a priestly tribe (Jos 18:7) without any specific land area allotted to it—the Lord was their portion. According to the description in Numbers they have liturgical duties, serving the priests, and are entitled to a tithe from the rest of the tribes. Although they have no plot of land like the other tribes, they were allotted certain areas in each tribe for residence and cultivation (Num 20–21). Among these holdings were the so-called "six cities of refuge." You may recall that the idea of "cities of refuge" has had a long life. In the medieval period churches served as places of refuge, and this idea has been invoked in the past several years in America to protect the lives of many people. The purpose of this institution was to protect an alleged killer from a *go'el* (avenger) who might carry out blood vengeance before a trial could be held (cf. Ex 21:12–14). But to return to the levites and the priests: Supposedly within the levites Aaron and his descendants were given the priestly prerogatives (Ex 29:9). But these few cannot account for all the complicated data in the Old Testament. For one thing, the levites seem to be considered priests and to exercise priestly functions at various sanctuaries. Deuteronomy makes no distinction between them and the priesthood, but speaks of "levitical priests" (e.g., 18:1–8). In his idealistic plan for the future (chaps. 40–48) Ezekiel demotes the levites, as it were, and they become merely ministers in the sanctuary (Ez 44:9–14). In the post-exilic period the office of high priest reaches its ascendancy. Although the Jews do not obtain independence, it is the high priest who is considered to be the effective leader, and outside powers deal with him.

Q. 38. I have heard of kosher food laws that govern the eating habits of many Jews today; do they have their origins in the laws of Leviticus?

One may speak of origins perhaps, but the full development of these laws came with the rabbis, and the details are to be found in the Mishna and Talmud. Here I would like to point out a few basic ideas that help us to understand something of the spirit behind these laws. One of the most important regulations regards blood, e.g., Lev 17:10, where life, blood and sacrifice are bound together: "I set my face against the one who eats blood....For the life of the flesh is in the blood....As life, it is blood that makes atonement." The basic reason is the association of life and blood, asserted often in the Bible.

In the code of the covenant, we read that "you shall not boil a kid in its mother's milk" (Ex 23:19; repeated in Dt 14:21). Various theories have been put forth to explain the literal historical sense of this passage (does it refer to some Canaanite religious practice?), but we remain in the dark. However, it became the basis for the Jewish practice of not eating meat along with dairy products. This is not the place to enlarge on later Jewish culinary habits that grew up over the centuries. The point to be emphasized is that food is not something that is taken for granted. It has religious significance. One not only thanks God for it, but the actual eating is seen as grounded in religious duty. Perhaps for a Catholic it may be likened to the old practice of abstinence from meat on Friday, a Church law that was eventually changed.

Q. 39. Would you explain the meaning of purity and impurity as these words are used in the Old Testament?

It is important first of all to emphasize that these terms have nothing to do per se with sex, nor do they deal with actions of immoral conduct. Rather, they incorporate basic primitive ideas about contact among living things and humans and even "holy things." The basic idea is that physical contact can render one *ritually* pure or impure. This means that one was qualified or not qualified to perform or share in certain liturgical actions. Place and space were holy, and called for a corresponding state (see Q. 40). Thus, the priest had to be ritually pure to perform sacrificial duties. Moreover, both purity and impurity were communicable. Thus the priest had also to be "desacralized," as it were, by a change of clothes before returning to normal human affairs. The same mentality lies behind the phrase "soil the hands," with reference to the sacred books of the Bible. If they "soil the hands" they are the holy books (other books do not have that effect). The meaning of "soil" is contrary to our usage, but it points to the fact that holiness is communicable. It should be kept in mind therefore that these laws deal not with intrinsic moral wrong or righteousness, but rather with an external state. Much of the legislation goes back so far in time, and was also probably borrowed, that the symbolism is difficult to comprehend. In the *NIB*, I, p. 281, Gary Anderson puts it this way: "Although no explanation has been offered that makes sense of every purity law, the one common thread that does seem to follow through most of them is the notion of human mortality…By the act of maintaining these physical rules and boundaries, Israel was made to reflect on the high demands of access to God."

The laws in Leviticus 11–16 preserve such legislation, and we may instance some of these by way of example. Perhaps the best known to Christian readers are the prescriptions concerning "leprosy" about which one reads also in the New Testament (Mt 8:1–4). Biblical leprosy does not indicate what we know as the grievous "Hansen's disease." It is used in a broad sense to indicate various types of skin eruptions. Moreover, clothes can be affected; mold and mildew account for "leprosy" of clothes. Likewise, even a building (Lev 14:34–53) can have a leprosy (not merely by contact with a leper), in that it can manifest blemishes that need to be removed. Personal leprosy was serious enough to ostracize a person from general society. Such an individual had to present himself to a priest for a decision. The priest was not a medical physician. He determined simply whether the person was infected or healed. In the former case elaborate purificatory ceremonies were prescribed before a normal life could be resumed. Closely related to the category of pure and impure is that of clean and unclean. Perhaps the best known example is the list of clean and unclean animals in Leviticus 11: animals that can be eaten, and those that are not to be eaten. It is not possible to determine the reasons behind the distinction, and the classification may seem bizarre to the modern reader. These laws are invested with a symbolism we cannot capture. This same chapter ends with the words, "I am the Lord your God…be holy for I am holy.…I am the Lord who brought you up from the land of Egypt to be your God; you shall be holy as I am holy" (Lev 11:24–45).

Q. 40. What is meant by "holiness"?

Perhaps the average person limits the notion of holiness to ethical holiness, to moral purity, to saintliness. The biblical notion of holiness includes this, but it is in fact far richer. The etymology of the root, q-d-sh, has to do with separation, setting apart. While this notion might appear rather inadequate at first sight, there is a lot to be said for it. Essentially, it puts God in a class apart. The Lord is separate, different, wholly other, belonging to another level of existence. Hence it is appropriate that in the inaugural vision of Isaiah (6:3) the Seraphim should call out, "qadosh, qadosh, qadosh, the Lord God of hosts!" One may note on this occasion that Isaiah is particularly aware of the ethical dimensions in his reaction, "a man of unclean lips," and one of the Seraphim touches his lips with a live coal to purge away his sin and guilt. But the true notion of biblical holiness is that the Lord alone is holy. "Holy" human beings are called "faithful" (*chasidim*) or "fearing God" (such as Job), or by some other synonym.

Leviticus carries the striking affirmation, "You shall be holy, for I the Lord your God am holy" (19:2), and this is matched by the powerful "I am the Lord your God," repeatedly echoed after the series of commands given in this chapter. You may also recall that in Mark 12:31 Jesus presents Leviticus 19:18b as the "second" commandment—like to the first, of loving the Lord totally, taken from Deuteronomy 6:4. Chapter 19 of Leviticus makes explicit what holiness meant for the Israelite. Following the command to be holy is a series of prescriptions, several of them familiar to us from the Ten Commandments, but many are not, e.g., leaving the gleanings of a field to be picked up by the poor. It is clear that Israel will be holy insofar as it keeps the commandments of the Lord, thus making itself worthy of being in the presence of the One who was called "the Holy One of Israel" (a favorite expression in the book of Isaiah; cf. 1:4; 14:10).

Perhaps the best way of conceiving biblical holiness is to recognize that only the Lord has this mysterious quality, and persons and things participate in it to a limited extent. Thus the members of the heavenly court constitute the divine family; they are "the holy ones." The Lord's residence in the Jerusalem Temple made that holy, and here too are degrees: the "holy of holies" contained the Ark, and the "holy place" was an extension of it. All utensils used in the liturgical services were holy precisely because of their use. Human beings were holy to the extent to which they approached God, the center of holiness; thus the priest and high priest. There was, therefore, a "sphere of holiness"—exemplified in the command to Moses that he remove his sandals from his feet because he was standing on holy ground (Ex 3:5). That was as important as any specific ethical standard because it "grounded," so to speak, the whole notion of holiness in the Lord. Anything else was a derived holiness. And even if ethical conduct was demanded by the Lord (e.g., Ps 15), one needed to remember the possibility of self-deception. As Proverbs 21:2 (*NRSV*) puts it, "All deeds are right in the sight of the doer, but the Lord weighs the heart" (cf. Prv 16:2). The Old Testament emphasis on the holiness of the Lord and the derived holiness of anything else remains a basic insight for the Christian as well.

Q. 41. Does the feast of Yom Kippur that Jews celebrate today have its origins in the Torah?

Yom Kippur ("the Day of Atonement") is one of the most important Jewish feasts, and while it has also been formed by the traditions in the Talmud, its biblical origins are clear from Leviticus. There we learn (Lev 16:29–34; 23:26–32; see also Num 29:7–11) that it is a day of total self-denial, and a "sabbath of complete rest." The purpose is atonement, for the sanctuary and altar, as well as for all the people. The anointed (high) priest carried out certain sacrifices. It is specified as a perpetual feast, to be celebrated on the 10th of Tishri (September-October), the seventh month of the year. Only on this day was the priest allowed to enter the holy of holies (where the Ark of the Covenant was). He sacrificed a goat for the sins of the community and sprinkled the blood on the *kapporet* (or "mercy seat," a golden slab on top of the Ark). Leviticus 16 specifies that two goats were chosen and lots were cast to determine the one for the Lord and the one for Azazel (probably a demon who dwelt in the desert with other devils—it was a common biblical notion that demons dwelt there). There was an imposition of hands on the head of the goat for Azazel by the priest—a symbolic action transferring the sins of the community. Then, carrying the sins of the people, it was led out into the desert, but not slain. It is not known just when this feast of the Day of Atonement was instituted, but it remains a solemn holy day among the Jewish people. The text of Leviticus is very emphatic in describing it as a total sabbath and a perpetual feast.

Q. 42. Why is anointing so frequent in biblical ritual?

Probably each rite had its own rationale for anointing, and this is really not explained. The appropriateness and importance of anointing is simply taken for granted. The secular use of precious oils after bathing was customary, when it could be afforded, in the ancient Near East. It also seems to be the usual amenity offered to a guest, as may be inferred from the words of Jesus to Simon in Luke 7:36–46. In contrast to Simon's cold reception (no water for the feet, no oil for anointing the head), a woman enters the house and bathes his feet with ointment (and her tears).

Our interest here is in the religious significance of anointing. Although we think of it perhaps particularly in terms of anointing of priests, the primary figure who was "the anointed" is the king. The anointing of the king made him a sacral figure, as we remember from David's words I Samuel 24:6, when he cut off a corner of Saul's cloak.

Although his comrades had in mind much more violent treatment, David's conscience bothers him: "The Lord forbid that I should do this to my lord, the anointed, putting out my hand against him, for he is the anointed of the Lord!" It was the king who was the anointed one par excellence; the anointing of the high priests in the post-exilic period was derived from the royal practice.

The word "anointed" is a translation of *christos* in Greek, *mashiah* in Hebrew, which is rendered messiah in English. Note the small "m," because in the Old Testament the word refers most often to the reigning king (an unusual case is Isaiah 45:1, where it is used of Cyrus). As time went on, the term became more specialized so that in the New Testament there is question of *the* Messiah, or the Son of David, the fulfillment of the oracle of Nathan to David in 2 Samuel 7:11–17.

Q. 43. Are the vows mentioned in the Old Testament the same kind of vows as Christians make, for example, in religious orders?

Perhaps the best answer is that a vow is a vow, no matter who makes it. There can be, of course, varying degrees of solemnity and intention, and the matter of the vows can vary considerably. For example, a vow of chastity is well nigh inconceivable in the Old Testament because of the high regard that Israel had for the gift of children. A childless woman was to be pitied (think of Hannah in 1 Samuel 1). There are many references to vows throughout the psalter (cf., e.g., Pss 22:26; 50:14; 61:6, etc.). Thus, one would pray for something such as deliverance from sickness or whatever, and this prayer would be accompanied by a promise/vow to give something in return—an offering in the temple, or the like. This was not as mechanical or as mercenary as it looks. It was an earnest of the seriousness of the prayer. The most famous vow is that of Jephthah in Judges 11:29–40, where he vowed to sacrifice whatever came from his house if he returned from war with a victory over the Ammonites. Alas, he did return, and it was his daughter that he met. The correct interpretation has nothing to do with a vow of virginity (cf.11:38), as some ancients claimed. Jephthah thought that he could not escape his responsibility for making the vow, so he carried it out.

In the Old Testament vows are conditional (e.g., Jephthah, if he returns victorious). And one dedicates something to the sanctuary

(Hannah offers Samuel as a nazirite). According to Leviticus 27:1–8, the vow could be redeemed by monetary payment. Sacrifices were the usual means of fulfillment of vows (Lev 22:17–30). Vows were not to be taken lightly as the words of Qoheleth make clear: "When you make a vow to God, do not be slow to fulfill it, for he has no pleasure in fools. Fulfill what you vow! It is better for you not to vow, than to vow and not fulfill it" (Eccl 5:3–4). However, vows made by women could be annulled by a father (for a daughter) or a husband (for the wife), as Numbers 30:2–17 indicates. This reflects the subordinate position of women in the culture of the ancient Near East.

The nazirite vow that I just mentioned deserves more detailed remarks. It was a vow that involved three promises: to abstain from the fruit of the vine and other intoxicants, never to cut one's hair during the time of the vow, never to go near a corpse (such an action would render a person "ritually impure"), even though it be a member of one's immediate family (Num 6:1–8). These three obligations were to be strictly observed during the period of the vow, for the person was considered as holy, dedicated to the Lord. The most famous nazirite is Samuel (it would appear that his mother, Hannah, dedicated him before birth as a perpetual nazirite until death; 1 Sam 1:11). Another is Samson (Jgs 17:7; cf. 16:17). In the New Testament there is an indication that John the Baptist was a nazirite: "He will be great before the Lord, and will drink no wine or strong drink" (Lk 1:15). Some think that the designation of Jesus as a "Nazorean" in Matthew 2:23 suggests that he was considered to be a nazirite; although there is no mention of vows, he is "dedicated" to the Lord. One may conclude that there are many biblical precedents for Christian vows; the basic similarity lies in the binding promise to perform some action in honor of God.

Q. 44. Why are the first-born, whether humans or produce of the earth or animals, singled out for such attention in the Old Testament?

It is not possible to give the theoretical reasons behind such practices; they were simply carried out, and not only by Israelites, for they are also found in other cultures. A typical example is Laban's reply to Jacob's complaint at not receiving Rachel as his wife: "It is not the prac-

tice in our country to give the younger before the first-born" (Gen
29:26). The inheritance of the first-born in a family was a double portion, e.g., twice what each of his brothers received. There was a practical
reason at work here; daughters would marry and leave the family, but
the males were considered the mainstay since they perpetuated the family line and the inheritance. One may conjecture that offering the
firstlings of the flock or the first-fruits of the earth was done in order to
secure blessings, especially fertility, upon the owner's possessions.

The issue of child sacrifice was already mentioned (Q. 17, the case
of Isaac), and many think that one purpose of Genesis 22 is to rule out
such a practice. Some would consider the legislation in Israel as originally including the literal sacrifice of the first-born. The Lord tells Moses in
Exodus 13:1–2: "Consecrate to me all the first-born; whatever first opens
the womb among the Israelites, man or beast, is mine." Then there is the
ambiguous question in Micah 6:7, "Shall I give my first-born for my
transgression, the fruit of my womb for my own sin?" Exodus 34:19–20
contains more legislation about the first-born, and it explicitly says that
"you shall redeem (ga'al) all the first-born of your sons." Although
Exodus 22:28–29 legislates that they are to "give" the first-born of
humans in the same context as "giving" the first-born of cattle and flocks,
it is generally presumed that the exception for humans (redemption) is to
be understood. Be that as it may, it is clear that redemption of the first-
born of humans is standard Old Testament practice.

It is the standard practice in the New Testament as well. Jesus is
presented in the Temple and Luke quotes Exodus 13:2, "Every first-
born male is considered consecrated to the Lord." The "redemption"
that was allowed for the poor was "a pair of doves or two young
pigeons" (Lk 2:23–24).

Q. 45. Is there any connection between the Church practice of the "churching of women" and the purification of Mary, to which Q. 44 refers?

That's a difficult question to answer because of the long history
that lies behind the feast of the purification. Let us first consider the
"purification." Leviticus 12:1–8 specifies that the mother of a male child
remains ritually unclean for seven days, and there follows a period of

"blood purification" for thirty-three days. Finally, a purification offering is made—for the poor, a pair of turtle doves or two young pigeons. Some form of this ritual lies behind Mary's purification in Luke 2:22—24. She and her husband are devout Jews ready to fulfill the requirements of the law. In the Temple, stress is laid upon the presenting of the child to the Lord (Lk 23:22), but the "redeeming" of the first-born is as specified in Exodus 13:1–2. The verses in Luke seem like an introduction to the climactic scenes with Simeon and Anna that follow.

The Lucan narrative has given rise to several feasts in the history of the Christian Church. In the East under Justinian (d.565) there was celebrated the feast of the "Meeting of the Lord" with Simeon and Anna. There was also a feast of the Lord celebrated in Jerusalem at the time of the famous pilgrim, Egeria or Etheria (end of the fourth century). Luke 2:23 gave rise to a procession of lights in Jerusalem in the fifth century (our later Candlemas). The feast finally entered the Gelasian Sacramentary as "the Purification of Holy Mary," and credit is given to Egeria.

I bring up these historical notices as background to the notion of the "churching of women." They show how tortuous is the history of feasts, but I think it is part of your question. We are now talking about a custom that sprang up in the church in imitation of the biblical events we have just rehearsed from Leviticus and Luke. The custom seems to go back to medieval times, and it stressed the thanksgiving after childbirth. But some of the ancient liturgical prayers, I have been told, show a residual notion of the "impurity" (even if this was only ritual, a concept not readily understood by Christians). It should also be remembered that even the sacred and association with the sacred made one ritually unclean. In connection with the ritual of churching there may have been some influence of Jansenism, and also an attitude that deprecated any connection of religion with sex. One may recall in the not too distant past that Holy Communion was not considered "proper," as it were, after marital intercourse. Yet the prayers that have been used, in this century at least, for the ritual of "churching" were filled with thanksgiving and praise.

Q. 46. What is the meaning of "sacrifice"?

Not all would agree on one definition, because it is to be derived from the particular details that enter into the concrete action termed "sacrifice." Hence there is a wide variation in determining the meaning. It has been construed as a gift to a selfish if not inimical deity, or a substitution for a sinful human, or a meal for the god(s) and so forth. One may theorize in this fashion: although God possesses everything, and humans owe all that they have to God, they can go without certain things and give them back to God, as it were. In terms of sacralization, everything that belongs to God is holy, and we can "desacralize" what we give to God in order to enjoy all of creation. The text of Psalm 50:13–14 is pertinent here: "Were I hungry I would not tell you, for mine is the world and all that fills it. Do I eat the flesh of bulls or drink the blood of goats? Offer praise as your sacrifice to God..."(*NAB*). A sacrifice is worth whatever interior spirit is put into it; mere formalism or performance avails nothing.

As sincere and exalted as a sacrifice may be, it contains temptations for the loyal believer, and the Old Testament is not slow to point them out. The most cutting indictments of the ritual laws and of sacrifice come from the prophets and thus from the Lord. With bitter sarcasm Amos calls out to the people:

> Come to Bethel—and transgress;
>   to Gilgal—and multiply transgression;
> Bring your sacrifices every morning,
>   your tithes every three days;
> Bring a thank offering of leavened bread,
>   and proclaim freewill offerings,
>   for so you love to do, O people of Israel!
>   says the Lord your God (Am 4:4–5, *NRSV*).

The Lord announces in Hosea 6:6, "I desire steadfast love and not sacrifice, the knowledge of God rather than burnt offerings" (*NRSV*). In Isaiah 1:11–16 we read: "What care I for the number of your sacrifices?...In the blood of calves, lambs and goats I find no pleasure.... Trample my courts no more! Bring no more worthless offerings; your incense is loathsome to me. Though you pray the more, I will not listen....Wash yourselves clean" (*NAB*). These searing words were meant to purify the motives and interior spirit, not to abolish the sacrificial system. If there is no correspondence between exterior worship and exemplary conduct, worship is meaningless.

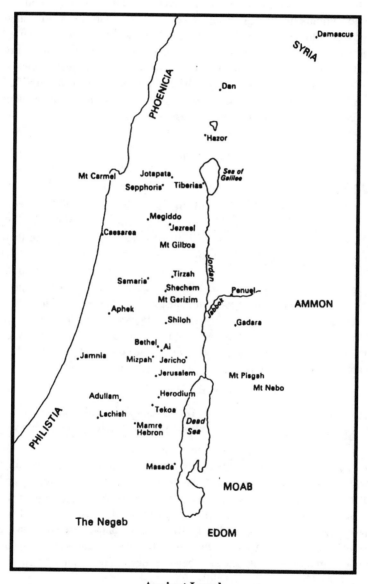

Ancient Israel

Incense forms part of Roman Catholic ritual, although it seems to be less commonly used after Vatican II. It finds a counterpart in the altar of incense that existed in the temple. Incense was also commonly used throughout the ancient Near East. It was usually mixed with several aromatic perfumes (cf. Ex 30:34–38), and its symbolism is best expressed in Psalm 141:2, "Let my prayer be incense before you, my uplifted hands an evening sacrifice." The biblical struggle to bring together prayer, sacrifice, and conduct remains also our struggle today.

NUMBERS/BEMIDBAR

Q. 47. Isn't "Numbers" a strange name for a biblical book?

Yes, it is, and it is derived from the Greco-Latin tradition (*arithmoi, numeri*) which has seized upon a prominent feature of the opening chapters: the census or numbering of the Israelites as they begin their trek from Sinai. The Hebrew title conveys the sense better: "in the desert," and that is exactly where the Israelites are and shall be until almost the very end of the book. When one hears of the "wilderness period" or the "desert wandering," one must turn to the book of Numbers to discover the many adventures of Israel after departing from Sinai. In some instances it repeats certain events related in Exodus, but it adds many more, especially the tensions within the community and the rebellion of the people in refusing to proceed into Canaan (chap. 14).

Q. 48. I seem to remember that David took up a census and was punished for it, but now isn't Moses told explicitly by the Lord to take up a census?

Your memory serves you right. But a census is an ambiguous thing; why is it taken up? In the case of David, he is planning on the security and also the extension of his kingdom (mainly in Transjordan). Even Joab, his trusted minister of war, calls this into question: why a census of all from Dan to Beer-sheba? This has been interpreted as a practical religious move on the part of Joab to ward off any possibility of the soldiers infringing on the required ritual purity and thus being subject to divine punishment (cf. Ex 30:12). For example, David's words to Ahimelech the priest justifies the eating of holy bread because his soldiers have refrained from intercourse (cf. Ex 19:15 and also Mt 12:3–4); they had to keep themselves ready for battle. On the other hand, there is the frequent admonition to trust in the Lord and not "in princes" (Pss 146:3; 118:9), and the prophet Isaiah scores King Ahaz for refusing to trust in the Lord (Is 7:10–13). Hence the census could be taken as a sign of human self-reliance and pride. However, in the case of the first census of Numbers, there is no sign of this. In fact, the number of men from the various tribes are to be arranged for the defense of the tabernacle, stationed at various points as the people proceeded through the desert. It is explicitly and frequently said in chapter 1 that the purpose is military, and the Lord gives a clear command to Moses (Num 1:2). The census will find a counterpart in chapter 26, but the purpose there is to underline the fact that it is a new generation that will enter Canaan; the rebellious generation has died out.

Q. 49. How is one to interpret the number of soldiers that the census yields?

This question can be raised about all the numbers given for the Israelites in the desert. It is calculated that some two million came out of Egypt, but the Sinai peninsula (as well as Palestine itself) could not sustain such a number. The number of men comes to over six hundred thousand according to the figures in Numbers 1. In Numbers 3:43 there are over twenty-two thousand first-born males. The fertility rate is simply too great; we are beyond the bounds of reality. But there is no sense in going on about numerical impossibilities. Several solutions have been preferred, and none of them have won any consensus. We can only say that the numbers are symbolic—and that is saying very little, because we have no idea what these symbols could have meant to ancient Israel. Perhaps one can say that such numbers magnify the greatness of the Lord in caring for the people. The P tradition is predominant in the chapters, but other traditions in the Pentateuch were comfortable with similar exaggerations.

Q. 50. Do you find anything in the data of Numbers 1–4 that makes it more than a tedious record of the distant past?

We must face the fact that numbers and data under any circumstances are tedious (you don't read the telephone directory for recreation). And if you exercise your preferences you will perhaps choose to move to another book in the Torah. But there is an important principle here, and that is the presence of God among the chosen people. That is what the desert tabernacle represents, and there can hardly be a more fundamental aspect to the religion of Israel. The patriarchs were favored by various theophanies, or limited appearances of God to them. On such occasions the place of the theophany became known as a holy place (remember Moses and the burning bush). The problem here is manifold, much more complicated than moderns, who perhaps take the presence of God for granted, realize. When Solomon dedicated the Temple (1 Kgs 8:27–28), his prayer caught the mystery of it all: "Will God really dwell on earth? Even heaven and the highest heaven cannot contain you, much less this Temple I have built"—the mystery of God's presence. The entire prayer testifies to this and to the graciousness of the Lord's being with the people as he was with the fathers (8:58). This presence came to a focus in the Ark of the Covenant, the divine "footstool," where the invisible Lord was enthroned between the cherubim, the guardians of the throne. The late P tradition had no blueprint of the desert tabernacle, even though its text betrays some archaic features. It is in the light of the Jerusalem Temple that it reconstructed this presence and the "proper" way for a desert trip. Priests and levites are on all four sides, with the military strength of the tribes surrounding them, three tribes on a side. I would remind you that the P terminology for the tabernacle is significant; it is the *mishkan*, or the tent that is pitched among the people by the Lord. Perhaps we belong to a culture that needs a deeper understanding of holy space.

Israel's understanding of holy space was that it was both dangerous and beneficent. It was dangerous because one's own ritual impurity could contaminate it and bring down some calamity, yet it was beneficent because of the presence of the Lord.

Q. 51. I read in Numbers about the ordeal for the errant wife; why isn't there an appropriate one for the errant husband?

I have no answer to that question, except to point out that in a patriarchal society the woman was regarded as the possession of the man. Recall how the tenth commandment admonishes the male not to covet his neighbor's house, wife, slave, etc., as though they were all on the same level. The ordeal itself (Num 5:11–31) seems to be a mixture of magic and ritual. Briefly, it amounts to this: the accused (or simply "suspected") woman takes an oath before the priest that she has not done wrong. He gives her "the water of bitterness" (in which the written words of the oath are contained) to drink. If she is telling the truth, nothing happens. If she is lying, her womb will discharge and she shall be an execration among her people. Death is the usual punishment for one who is guilty of adultery (whether the husband or the wife; cf. Lev 20:10; Dt 22:22–24). It is difficult for the modern reader to see the husband get off without penalty if the wife's innocence is proved by the ordeal.

Q. 52. What is the Aaronic or priestly blessing?

This is so called because it is described as the manner in which Aaron and his descendants are to bless the Israelite people. You are familiar with it because it has been adopted in the Christian liturgy also. At first sight it appears to be merely repetitive, saying the same thing in different ways. But that is the secret of parallelism in Hebrew poetry: each line, each verb in this case, extends the idea. It is not a case of simple repetition. It is worth repeating here:

> May the Lord bless you and keep you!
> May the Lord let his face shine upon you and be gracious to you!
> May the Lord look kindly upon you and give you peace!

There are two verbs in each line, and the second verb extends and enlarges the first. Blessing is quite common as a general term, and here it is sharpened and particularized by the "keeping" that Israel so desperately needs in the desert. The mention of the keeping or guarding of the Lord is frequent in the Bible. Psalm 121 is dominated by this notion: neither sunstroke nor the hex of the moon can harm Israel because the Lord guards the coming and going of the people (vv. 7–8). The Lord is conceived as wrapped in light (Ps 104:2), and the idea of the shining of the Lord's face is also frequent in the psalms (e.g., 31:16; 67:2, a harvest hymn, etc.). It is of course a sign of benevolence that the Lord lets some view of his overpowering radiance be seen. When the Lord shines upon anyone, intimacy follows. In the last line "look kindly" is literally "lift up his face," and is comparable to Psalm 4:7, "Lift up the light of your face upon us."

Opposed to this is the frequent "hiding the face" to indicate divine displeasure (Dt 31:18). The Hebrew word for peace (shalom) has entered many languages with various nuances. It means much more than the absence of quarreling or war. It indicates well-being and prosperity (and of course all this is understood to be God-given). It is remarkable how extensive and all-comprehensive the priestly blessing is. Moreover, it would be hard to imagine a more ecumenical prayer than this.

Q. 53. Is the Passover that is celebrated in Numbers 9 the same celebration as in Exodus 12?

It is the same feast, but there are differences in the ritual, as might be expected. A comparison between the two chapters is an example of the changes one must expect in law and in liturgy across time and changing conditions. In terms of time only about one year elapses before Israel departs from Sinai, but we must remember that the text in Numbers is later than the actual text in Exodus. Moreover the Exodus test describes the feast with all the tension and excitement that the origin of the feast calls for: the escape from Egypt. The blood of the lamb is to be daubed on the doorposts and lintel of the houses, and the lamb eaten with unleavened bread (this itself is a rite that was added later). Finally, it is to be eaten by all with their loins girded, sandals on feet and staff in hand in a hurried fashion—the flight from Egypt is upon them. In contrast, the celebration in Numbers 12 manifests a more relaxed mood. Thus, specific legislation about those who are ritually impure (12:6) is given; their observance of the Passover is postponed to the second month.

The beautiful passage which ends chapter 12 echoes the comments of Exodus 13:21–22 concerning the pillar of cloud by day and night. The two pillars are really one: the cloud leads by day but the radiance of the Lord within the cloud is the beacon for night travel. It was through the cloud/fire that the Lord threw a glance that panicked the Egyptian army (Ex 14:25). The very ending of the book of Exodus returns to this motif of the cloud/fire (Ex 40:34–38). In Num 9:15–23, the complete dependence of Israel upon the cloud/fire for its journey is repeated in detail. Now, however, it is over the tabernacle, and its movement indicates go, stop or stay (vv. 18, 20, 23). Once again we have another example of the (guiding) presence of God.

Q. 54. "Murmuring" in the desert was mentioned above in connection with the book of Exodus (Q. 30). Doesn't the book of Numbers describe a revolt (and many of them) in the desert?

You are right—the troubles after leaving Sinai, described especially in Numbers 11–14, 16–17, 20, are far more serious than the complaints that are voiced in Exodus 15–17. There the bitter waters of Marah were made potable, the yearning for the "fleshpots" was answered by manna and quail, and at Massah and Meribah water came from the rock. Running through these narratives is the idea of testing (Ex 15:25; 16:24; 17:7). The supreme example of rebellion against Moses (Ex 32:1, "We don't know what has happened to him") is the golden calf episode. There is no question about the wrath of Moses, but his prayer in Exodus 32:11–14 is a remarkable reply to the Lord's declaration that there will be a change in plans and the promise of a great nation will be shifted to Moses and his descendants (32:10). Moses digs deep into Israel's memories: What will the Egyptians say? What about the promises sworn to Abraham, Isaac and Jacob? In Numbers 14:12 the Lord returns to the same point—to do away with Israel, and make of Moses a nation greater and more powerful. The impassioned intercession of Moses rises to greater heights. He not only invokes the rationalization of the Egyptians (the Lord was not able to save Israel, so they have been slaughtered), but he quotes the immortal lines of Exodus 34:6, "The Lord is slow to anger and abounding in love…" (14:13–19). The occasion is the refusal of the people to enter Canaan after the reconnoitering of the scouts. This is, of course, the supreme revolt: a rebellion punished by the forty years of wandering the desert.

Does Moses himself ever seem to lose control of the situation in his dialogue with the divinity? In Numbers 11:11 he makes a strong yet touching plea for himself: "Why have you treated your servant so badly? Why have I not found favor in your sight, that you lay the burden of all this people on me? Did I conceive all this people? Did I give birth to them, that you should say to me, 'Carry them in your bosom as a nurse carries a sucking child' to the land that you promised on oath to their ancestors? Where am I to get meat to give to all this people? For they come weeping to me and say, 'Give us meat to eat!' I am not able to carry all this people alone, for they are too heavy for me. If this is the way you are going to treat me, put me to death at once—if I have found favor in your sight—and do not let me see my misery" (Num 11:11–15, *NRSV*).

There are several personal revolts, such as those of Moses' own family against his authority (Miriam and Aaron, chap. 12), and those of certain ambitious Israelites (Korah, Dathan and Abiram, chaps. 16–17) who rebel against the authority of Moses and Aaron. But these are nothing compared to the refusal of the people to enter the promised land. You will recall that twelve "spies" (one from each tribe) reconnoiter the land of Canaan, and they return after forty days with reports of a land flowing with milk and honey but also populated by strong peoples and fortified towns, typical enemies of Israel, such as the Amalekites. Only Caleb, among the scouts, urges the people to go up, but they refuse. It is on this occasion that Moses makes his impassioned plea to the Lord that has just been quoted above (Num 14:13–19). The punishment is that the desert generation shall *not* enter Canaan, but shall wander and die in the desert.

Q. 55. Why doesn't Moses enter the promised land?

That is one of the big secrets of the Pentateuch and of Israelite tradition. I think the correct answer is that this question was as puzzling to them as it is to us. Why? Because the question is brought up, implicitly at least, several times, and a clear answer never emerges. Let me illustrate. In Q. 30 I indicated one point of view: Moses' striking of the rock twice is the customary explanation. Numbers 20:2–14 cannot be interpreted that way. It is a doublet to Exodus 17:1–7: another typical complaint—no water to drink. The Lord comes to the rescue of Moses and Aaron; they are to take the well-known staff, and before all the community "speak" (i.e., command) to the rock and it will yield the water. Accordingly, Moses addresses the assembled congregation, and begins: "Listen, you rebels, shall we take water for you out of this rock?" Moses strikes the rock twice with the staff and the water is provided. There is no angry reaction from the Lord, but merely the rather dry and jejune observation: "Because you did not trust in me to show my holiness before the eyes of the Israelites, therefore you shall not lead this people into the land I have given them." The next verse (13) is an etiological explanation of the place name: "These are the waters of Meribah where the Israelites quarreled with the Lord and by which he manifested his holiness." In an apparent doublet in Exodus 17:6–7 there is no mention of striking the rock twice, and the event is interpreted as Israel testing the Lord. This casual explanation given by the Lord is reiterated in Numbers 20:24 at the death of Aaron; he has not entered the promised land because of the rebellion of Aaron and Moses at Meribah. In Numbers 27:12–14 the same reason is given: while Moses is told to go up the Abarim mountain range to get a good view of the land, he is reminded that this will be his only view because he and Aaron disobeyed the word of the Lord: "You did not show forth my holiness before their (the people's) eyes at the waters" (v. 14). No further explanation of the obscure "show forth my holiness" is given. The waters are identified as those of Meribath-kadesh in the desert of Zin. The event itself remains mysterious. It is gratuitous to suppose that hitting the rock twice presupposes a lack of faith.

When one turns to the book of Deuteronomy, a different slant is given to the prohibition. In the style of Moses' "speeches," we hear him saying to the people that the Lord was angry with him "on your account" (Dt 1:37). The blame lies with the people! After an impassioned plea by Moses to cross over the Jordan "at that time" (when the east bank of the Jordan had been secured, Dt 3:8–22), he receives a gruff answer from the Lord: he is never to bring up the matter again. But the reason remains the same: "on your account" (3:26). The same version is found again, and on the lips of Moses speaking to the people, in 4:22. There is an unmistakable plaintive note in his words: "I am to die in this land without crossing over the Jordan, but you are going to cross over...." In Deuteronomy 32:48–52 there is a substantial restatement of Numbers 27:12–14: Moses and Aaron (who has already died) cannot enter Canaan because they both "broke faith" with the Lord and did not show forth his holiness among the Israelites. If we follow the traditions within the Pentateuch, it seems rather clear that the priestly version places the blame (without ever being really specific) upon Moses, whereas the Deuteronomic view lays the blame on the people (Deuteronomy 32:48–52 is obviously to be attributed to P). With unabashed frankness the editor(s) of the Pentateuch give two different versions to explain why Moses never crossed the Jordan—but leaving both reasons shrouded in a mysterious generalization.

Q. 56. How do you explain the episode of the bronze serpent (Num 21:4–9)?

As you recall the incident in Numbers 21:4–9, this is another instance of the complaint of the people about the food in the desert. In punishment the Lord sends saraph (fiery?) serpents that bite and kill many Israelites. The people acknowledge their sinful rebellion and implore Moses' intercession. Along with his prayer Moses makes a saraph at the bidding of the Lord and sets it upon a pole—whoever looks upon this "serpent of bronze" will be healed from the snake-bite. This is usually described by scholars as an episode of sympathetic magic, that is, the belief that certain things or actions have an affinity, and one of them can be influenced by its co-equal. In this case, the snake-bite is cured by the image of the snake. This episode has acquired particular importance because of the bronze serpent (called Nehushtan) that Hezekiah eliminated from the Jerusalem Temple (2 Kgs 18:4). The story in Numbers seems to give the etiology of this "bronze serpent." The episode is referred to again in later tradition. The author of the Wisdom of Solomon is anxious to see a higher meaning. The image was a sign of salvation, reminding the Israelites of the law; they were saved, "not by what they saw," but by God, the Savior of all (Wis 16:6–7). Finally, in John 3:14 one finds a typological connection between the lifting up of the serpent and the lifting up (resurrection and ascension) of Jesus.

Q. 57. Don't you find it strange that the story of Balaam and his ass got into Bible?

That question might be directed at many other parts of the Bible! It all depends upon the meaning of the word "strange." Perhaps you are referring to the fact that there is an animal that talks. But that is not unheard of—think of the wily serpent and all the talk it gives out with in Genesis 3. In literary terms we usually think of stories with talking animals as fables, and there is no reason why that kind of literary genre should not appear in the Bible. In both cases there is a serious theological undercurrent. The conversation of the serpent with the woman is one of the most adroit descriptions of how human beings can be tricked; the twists and turns of the conversation suggest a literary skill that is far from ordinary.

What about Balaam and his ass? This incident is situated in a very threatening narrative. Balak, king of Moab, is disturbed at the military power displayed by the Israelites, and he hires Balaam, a (presumably) well-known spellbinder, to put a hex upon them. He is not an Israelite, and his origins are not clear (Amaw in 22:5 is otherwise unknown, but here it is associated with the Euphrates). When he is contacted by Balak's emissaries to place a curse upon Israel his reaction is unusual; he claims that he must consult with the Lord, the God of Israel. The consultation does not bode well for Balak. Balaam is not to curse Israel, and so Balaam refuses. Balak makes another offer and again Balaam consults the Lord. Now Balaam agrees but understands from God that he will say only what he is told to say. It is at this point that the clever episode of the donkey takes place (22:22–35). What does this fable do? It satirizes a seer who cannot see (Balaam cannot see the angel of God blocking the path) and credits an animal who *can* see. Three times the donkey saves him until finally the eyes of Balaam are really opened and he is ready to turn back. Then he receives the puzzling command to forge ahead but to say only what the Lord tells him to say.

There is an unmistakable comic air to all this because three times Balaam has to bless Israel when he is hired to curse them. Balak storms at him and there is a kind of ritual going on between them (compare 23:11–12, 25–26; 24:11–14). The most famous lines have to do with the star coming out of Jacob, the scepter rising out of Israel, to be victorious (24:17, which suggests a reference to the expansion of the kingdom under David, but the words also came to be understood in an eschatological and messianic sense).

Balaam's fame is also registered in a 1967 discovery by archeologists at tell Deir Alla in Transjordan. Aramaic texts on plaster panels refer to him as a "seer of the gods," and they relate a calamity that he foresees. Elsewhere in Israelite tradition Balaam acquires a bad reputation (e.g., Num 31:16; Jos 13:22).

Q. 58. What were the Urim referred to in the commissioning of Joshua as the successor to Moses?

The issue is: Who is to succeed Moses? In Numbers 27:16 Moses asks the Lord to appoint a leader so that the people be not like "sheep without a shepherd." But first Eleazar the priest (Aaron has died) shall inquire about the decision of the Urim concerning this action. The reference goes back to the description of the garments of the high priest in Exodus 28:29–30. In the breastplate were contained "Urim and Thummim," presumably some kind of stones used to determine the divine will (by color, or size?). These are referred to several times in later history when a decision from the Lord is sought directly (1 Sam 14:41–43). It is when Saul receives no answer by the Urim that he has recourse to the medium at Endor (1 Sam 28:6). There is no adequate translation of the terms; hence the transliteration, Urim and Thummim, is used. This was translated by Jerome as "lux et veritas," light and truth, and the Latin phrase became the motto of Yale University. The basis for the casting of lots was the belief in the causality or agency of God behind everything that occurs. Proverbs 16:33 describes this well:

> When the lot is cast into the lap,
>   its decision depends entirely on the Lord (*NAB*).

This action was not regarded as ruled by chance, and the casting of lots is continued in Acts when Matthias is chosen instead of Barsabbas as an apostle (Acts 1:26). The accompanying prayer is worthy of note: "Lord, you know the hearts of all; show which one of these two you have chosen..." (1:24).

The succession of Joshua was a vital element in Israelite tradition. It has been pointed out that Joshua repeats many of the actions of Moses: sending out spies (Num 13; Jos 2); crossing waters on dry ground (Ex 14; Jos 3); removing shoes because of holy ground (Ex 3:5; Jos 5:15); see M. Coogan in *NJBC*, pp. 110–11.

Q. 59. Is Transjordan (the highlands on the eastern side of the river) considered the promised land?

Strictly speaking, it is the land of Canaan that is the goal of Israel's journey. They attempt to penetrate from the south after rejecting the advice of Joshua and Caleb and they fail (Num 14:26–45). Eventually they go up by way of the "King's Highway" (Num 21:22) on the eastern side of the Jordan River and go as far north as Bashan, defeating king Og at Edrei (22:33). This proved to be tempting to Reuben and Gad with their large cattle possessions, and they coveted the fertile area of Gilead. To their request to settle there and dispense with the crossing of the Jordan, Moses gives a sharp answer and likens their conduct to the refusal of the people to follow Joshua and Caleb. They hasten to reassure him that they will fight for Israelite possession of Canaan, but they want the Transjordan for their portion. Moses finally accedes to their request, and they are joined by half of the tribe of Manasseh (chap. 32). In this sense the area belongs to the promised land, and of course, it remains part of the northern kingdom until the Assyrian conquest.

Far more important than these geographical considerations is what may be called the theology of the land (cf. W. D. Davies, *The Gospel and the Land* [Berkeley, 1974] 15–35. True, the land of Canaan is the promised land—promised to Abraham and his descendants (Gen 12:1–3, 15–18). But before that it is the land of *yhwh*. This is clearly stated in Leviticus 25:23 and elsewhere. It is also implied by the fact that the land is a *gift* to Israel. It was not Israel's prowess in war; rather, the Lord gave them the land (Ps 44:2–4). The Lord's ownership also accounts for the apportioning of the land by means of the lot; no one had any title to it. Hence too the offering of first-fruits was simply giving back to the Lord, symbolically, what was rightfully his. For this reason the land observed a "sabbath to the Lord," a sabbath of complete rest when the land lay fallow (Lev 25:2–5). For this reason also, it can be called a "holy land," although the phrase is not biblical. Holiness belongs to the Lord. The land somehow participates in this holiness, since it is a divine possession, so close to God; the contagion of holiness affects the land. Numbers 35:34 puts it this way: "You shall not defile the land in which you live, in which I myself dwell, for I the Lord dwell among the people of Israel." The association of the land and the moral life of Israel is found many times, especially among the prophets: "For the earth was polluted under its inhabitants, because they transgressed the laws, violated the statutes, broke the eternal covenant" (Is 24:4–5; cf. Am 1:2). Pollution or defilement of the land is a major disaster (Lev 19:29; Dt 21:23).

Q. 60. I remember a liturgical reading about two men with the colorful names Eldad and Medad. Were they important?

They were indeed! The reading is in the B cycle for the 26th Sunday of the Year, and is taken from Numbers 11:25–29. The background consists in the complaint of the people (Where's the meat?) and Moses' desperate plea to the Lord (Num 11:11–15, quoted above in Q. 54 about desert "murmuring"). The Lord commands Moses to gather together seventy of the elders to the Tent of Meeting; there the Lord will take of Moses' spirit and put it on them—thus Moses will not be alone in bearing the burden of the people, and he is authorized to tell the people that they will indeed have meat—for a month(!), enough to sicken them. Moses is incredulous: meat for six hundred thousand men? The Lord's reply is harsh: "Is the hand (power) of the Lord too short for this?" Then he takes Moses' spirit and puts it upon them. They "prophesy," i.e., they display the possession of the spirit, a kind of ecstatic manifestation exemplified in Saul (1 Sam 10:1–13) and in Ezekiel (1:28; 2:22, etc.) and several others. It is not said what the reaction of the people is to this. However two of the elders had remained in the camp, and had not been present when the rest of their group had received of Moses' spirit. These were Eldad and Medad (their names seem linked etymologically to the love of God). But the spirit now comes upon them and they also "prophesy." Joshua takes this amiss and tries to have Moses stop them. Then a classic answer: "Are you jealous on account of me? Would that all the people of the Lord were prophets, that the Lord would put his spirit upon them" (11:29). Moses seems to recognize that it was not his spirit, but the spirit of the Lord that came directly upon them. Free spirit that he is, Moses approves their conduct, as against the attitude of Joshua who was perhaps concerned about Moses' authority, or was simply a stickler for law and order. This incident could have been lost in the midst of the story about the abundant quail, which continues in 11:13ff. Fortunately it was preserved and woven into these events that occurred at Kibroth-hattaavah ("graves of craving"). Eldad and Medad are important in themselves as recipients of the divine spirit, and the reaction of Moses to this is exemplary.

Q. 61. Why is there such detail in the prescriptions concerning the fashioning of clothes, e.g., the tassels on cloaks?

You are referring to the instructions given in Numbers 5:37–41. I really can't answer your question with certainty, but I would remind you that it forms part of a pattern. You may recall that stirring recommendation of Deuteronomy 6:8–9 in which the command is given concerning the words spoken by Moses "today": "Bind them on your wrist as a sign and let them be as a frontlet on your forehead. Write them on the doorposts of your houses and on your gates." This injunction is the basis for the Jewish observances you may already know: phylacteries, frontlets, and the mezuza at the entrance of a house, all of them inscribed with certain verses of the Pentateuch and especially Deuteronomy 6. They are reminders of God and the divine will. Perhaps you have seen the beautiful prayer shawls that are donned by Jews as an aid to their devotion. The ideal is expressed very well in Numbers 15:39–41: "When you look at the fringe, you will remember all the commandments of the Lord that are to be kept, so that you do not go wantonly astray after the desires of your hearts and your eyes. Thus you will remember to keep all my commandments and be holy to your God. I am the Lord your God who brought you out of the land of Egypt—I, the Lord your God."

In his JPS commentary on Numbers (excursus 38) J. Milgrom also points out the symbolism of the hem of an outer robe; it is a kind of extension of the owner's personality. From this point of view, David's penitent concern over having cut off the hem of Saul's garment takes on added meaning (1 Sam 24:5–6). However, the religious meaning is uppermost. The practice may be likened to the wearing of special apparel at religious services in various branches of Christianity. Even if these garments can be traced back to "ordinary" dress of past centuries, they have been invested with religious significance.

Q. 62. What did it mean for a person to be "cut off"?

You are referring to a punishment that is frequently mentioned in the Torah. Thus, whoever eats leavened bread during the Passover is to be "cut off" (Ex 12:15). Profaning the sabbath merits death, and parallel to this statement is the verdict that anyone who works on the sabbath shall be "cut off from among the people" (Ex 31:14). In Numbers 15:27–31 there is a recognition of the difference between inadvertent wrongdoing and action "with a high hand." This latter phrase is used of the forthright and defiant departure of Israel from Egypt (Ex 14:8; Num 33:3). If one were to proceed against God "with a high hand," this would be a kind of declaration of war. Such a person is to be "cut off." There are many other references to being cut off (twenty-one times in all in the

Torah). The ambiguity of the word arises from two possibilities: it can mean a divine penalty (God will extirpate his line of progeny), or it can be a death penalty by some kind of execution (see Numbers 15:30–36 for death by stoning for one who breaks the sabbath).

Q. 63. Would you explain the meaning of the (resident) alien, or *ger*, that is referred to so often in the Pentateuch?

This "alien" is a stranger of a peculiar type. Such an alien is pro-tected by the community that received him or her as such, and is even given certain unusual rights by the community. One might say that this concept has had an interesting journey through the Bible. The patriarchs were aliens both in Canaan (Gen 14:13) and in Egypt (Ex 2:22). Even after they have received the land from God as a gift, they remain strangers, for the land belongs to God (Lev 25:23). But the normal use of the term is to designate a special a special class of non-Israelites who either singly or in enclaves were incorporated into Israel. They could hold no land, so they had to make their fortunes in various ways (in Dt 24:14–15 they are paired with the poor and needy and their wages must be paid to them). They were not incorporated into Israel on a spiritual plane. They could choose (but were not obligated) to observe the Passover, or to be circumcised, or offer sacrifice. But the laws of purity had to be observed by them, since otherwise the purity of the land would be affected. The term is also used in a metaphorical sense to suggest how transient one's life is (Ps 39:12), or to indicate a certain instability in one's situation (Ps 119:9).

Q. 64. What does it mean "to be gathered to one's people"?

The expression is a mild reference to death, and is used to describe the deaths of the great men of the Torah: Abraham (Gen 25:8), Ishmael (Gen 25:17), Jacob (Gen 49:33), Moses (Num 27:13); Dt 32:50) and Aaron (Num 20:24). Thus it occurs only in the Pentateuch and has an idiomatic meaning. Who are the "people" and what is meant by the "gathering"? The normal Old Testament view of death is that one died and resided in Sheol (see the description of Sheol in Job 3 and through-out the book). The "residence" in Sheol is not explained; one is just there, as David (2 Sam 12:23) realizes concerning his dead son: "I shall go to him, but he shall not return to me." Sheol was neither punitive nor rewarding. One was just "there," and it could be conceived as a relief (by Job in comparison with his earthly sufferings), or as an enemy (as frequently in the psalms, where Sheol/Death is personified as a power that pursues an individual). There was no rationalizing about "who" was in Sheol, i.e., the body was obviously in the grave, and the breath of life returned to God who gave it (Gen 2:7; Eccl 14:7). Life of course was better than death even if death was not a state of punishment. The distinctive note about Sheol in the psalms was that there was no longer any loving contact with the Lord: in Sheol who can praise you? (Pss 6:5; 30:9; 88:10, etc.).

It has been argued that gathering unto one's people or kin really implies an afterlife, where one is united with one's relatives in Sheol. It is an interim situation: after death but before burial. In view of the pervasive Old Testament view of Death/Sheol, this is difficult to accept. What could it mean? It seems to be a gentle way of referring to death. It is not an intermediate stage between death and burial. Rather, the expression reflects that remarkable resignation and acceptance of death that is characteristic of the Israelite people.

Q. 65. What was Phinehas famous for?

There are two well-known biblical characters by that name, one a hero and the other a rascal. The rascal is the son of Eli, the priest at Shiloh in the time of Samuel. He and his brother Hophni abused their office (1 Sam 2:12–17). After his death his wife gave birth to a son whom she named Ichabod (meaning "no glory"). It was a dire time for Israel since the Ark of the Covenant had been captured by the Philistines. The hero—and he is probably the one you have in mind—is mentioned in the book of Numbers (and several times elsewhere: Ps 106:28–31; Sir 45:23–24; 1 Mac 2:26, 54). He is singled out for a "zealous" deed that acquired for him and his line an eternal "covenant of peace." The occasion of his exploit was the seduction of the Israelites in sacrifices to the Baal of Peor (Num 25:1–13). The site of Peor remains unknown. It was probably another of the several shrines to Baal, and it was from a mountain of this name that Balaam delivered his third oracle

(Num 23:28). Here the Israelites were seduced to idolatry, involving sexual relations with Moabite women (Num 25:1–2). The Lord ordered the death of all the leaders of the people who were responsible for this. Somewhat ambiguously, Moses ordered the leaders to slay the Israelites who were involved in the rites. Now there is a climactic scene when an Israelite brings a Midianite woman to his family—before Moses and the whole community. Thereupon Phinehas spears the couple, presumably *in flagrante*, and the plague (previously unmentioned) ceases. In return, the Lord announces that Phinehas has turned aside the divine anger by his zeal. He is to receive a covenant of peace, pledge of an everlasting priesthood (presumably the Zadokites?) because of zeal for God and his ransoming of the Israelites by his deed.

Q. 66. I read recently that the year 2000 would be celebrated by the Catholic Church as a "jubilee year." Does this have any connection with the biblical year of jubilee?

The last Christian "jubilee year" I can remember is 1950, and the first was in 1300; and it has become an occasion of pilgrimage (physical or in spirit) to Rome and the major basilicas. The association with the biblical jubilee is merely nominal. There is a passing reference to the jubilee in Numbers 36:4 but the real legislation is contained in Leviticus 25:8–55 (see also Dt 15:1–9). According to Leviticus, there was to be a remission of debts and freeing of slaves every fiftieth year. The name itself is derived from *yobel*, perhaps meaning "ram," but having nothing to do with "jubilee" (Latin *jubilare*, to shout). Every seventh year was already marked for the manumission of Hebrew slaves (Ex 21:1–6) and rest for the land (Ex 23:10–11). Leviticus prescribes that there shall be seven weeks of years (seven times seven years, a forty-nine year cycle). Then on the Day of Atonement in the fiftieth year there shall be a jubilee, sanctified by proclaiming liberty to all. Everyone is to return to the family estate. During the fiftieth year there shall be no sowing or harvesting, and the release from debt for one's land is arranged. The basic principle is enunciated in Leviticus 25:23, "The land shall not be sold in perpetuity, for the land is mine; you are only aliens, tenants of mine." This regulation of land possession created a kind of social equilibrium and equity. The concern for the poor is remarkably progressive; they are to have the privileges of an alien or tenant so that they can live with the rich person (Lev 25:35–36). "Do not demand interest from your kin, whether by money or barter. Because you fear God, you shall let them live with you, lending no money at interest nor food at a profit. I the Lord am your God who brought you out of the land of Egypt to give you the land of Canaan, to be your God." But one must also remember the excoriations that the prophets delivered against the "haves" because they failed in their treatment of the "have nots." See also Leviticus 26:3–13 for the assurances given by the Lord to those who would live up to the ideals. The issue is not just material prosperity. It is the covenant, "I will be your God and you will be my people" (26:12). See also QQ. 59 and 63.

DEUTERONOMY/DEBARIM

Q. 67. Would you explain the names of this final book of the Torah?

As usual, the Jewish tradition takes the opening words of the book as the title, *'elleh haddebarim*, "These are the words," but it is shortened simply to *debarim* ("words"). This captures an important feature of the book: words, i.e., the words of Moses in three discourses. The English name again traces its origins back to the Latin *Deuteronomium* and the Greek *deuteronomion*. The Greek word ("second law") occurs in Deuteronomy 17:18, but it is an inexact translation of the Hebrew text which reads "copy of this law." By an odd twist, however, "second law" is not inept, in the sense that it describes a second covenant, as indicated in Deuteronomy 28:69 (ET 29:1): "These are the words of the covenant that the Lord commanded Moses with the Israelites, in addition to the covenant that he made with them at Sinai." The laws were given to Moses at Sinai, but it is in the plains of Moab (the area east of the Dead Sea) that they learn of the laws as interpreted in chapters 12–26, sometimes called the Deuteronomic code.

Q. 68. Would you comment on the structure of this book?

The basic observation to be made is that we pay attention to the editorial headings that have been supplied in 1:1–5; 4:44–49; 28:69 (ET 29:1); and 33:1. Thus, the book is made up of three speeches by Moses: (1) 1:6–4:40, in which he reviews the past history and experiences in the desert in order both to warn and to encourage the people as they stand ready to enter into the promised land. (2) The laying out of the order of society and general life style of the covenanted people in 4:49–28:69—the Ten Commandments and "the statutes and ordinances" that, as it were, explicate them. This is done with magnificent rhetoric about the Great Commandment (the first, that calls for total dedication to the Lord) in chapters 5–11, and in the preached law found in chapters 12–26. Chapters 27–28 lay out the blessings and curses that attach to the observance of the covenantal laws. (3) In 29:1–32:52 we have an emphasis on the covenant now being struck in Moab, and on the imminent death of Moses (along with the famous Song in Deuteronomy 32). The final chapters are like an appendix: the testament of Moses' blessing on the tribes (33), and an account of his death with an appraisal of this great man whom the Lord knew face to face (34:10).

It is important not to lose sight of the panorama that unfolds in the Pentateuch. In Exodus 19 Moses began to speak to the Israelites as covenant mediator communicating the will of God—and in Deuteronomy he is still speaking, as the three speeches indicate. The time span has been about forty years since Sinai, and much of the text has consisted of priestly legislation in Exodus, Leviticus and Numbers, and mediated by Moses ("and the Lord said to Moses," repeated countless times). In contrast, the speeches of Moses in Deuteronomy appear to be delivered all in one day.

Q. 69. How did this book come to be written?

Two factors help to determine the genesis and/or growth of the book. The first is the Deuteronomic style and its theological viewpoint. It is characterized by favorite words and phrases and by a strongly hortatory (as well as menacing) tone. One need merely read the book to capture this flavor. This points to a definite perspective or orientation. Can we find it elsewhere in the Bible? It appears in several of the "historical" books from Joshua to Kings. See, e.g., Joshua 1:1–12; 23:2–16; Judges 2:11–23; 1 Sam 12; 2 Kings 17:7–40. This theology has influenced these works, which are often termed the "Deuteronomistic history" (Joshua to Kings; sometimes abbreviated as Dtr). Secondly, the book can be tied in with the events related in 2 Kings 22–23. Here we read of the discovery of "the book of the law" (22:8) in the Temple during the course of the repairs that King Josiah had inaugurated. When the book is read aloud to the king, he is disturbed by its tone and message, and seeks confirmation of the work from Huldah, a prophetess. She informs him that the Lord will bring disaster upon Judah after him (he died in 609). The tie-in between this "book of the law" and Deuteronomy lies in the character of the reform that is carried out under Josiah: the removal of the worship of Baal, Asherah and astral deities (sun and moon), destruction of the high places and their idolatrous worship (extending north into what had been the kingdom of Israel), and centralization of worship in Jerusalem. 2 Kings 23:1–24 describes the reform in generous detail, and it ends with typical deuteronomistic praise of the king: "Before him there was no king like him who turned to the Lord with his whole heart, his whole soul, and whole might, according to the law of Moses..."(23:25). It has been claimed that the discovery of the book was just a pious fraud palmed off on king and people, but hardly anyone takes this charge seriously. The question arises: How long before Josiah would the "book of the law" have been written? this is difficult to answer. Was it the fruit of levitical preaching in the old northern kingdom of Israel (so G. von Rad) that gradually made its way to Jerusalem? Whatever the origins, the substance of the book must have extended into previous centuries. Already in the time of King Hezekiah (about 700) centralization of worship and removal of the high places appeared as orthodox policy (2 Kgs 18). In any case, this "book of the law" is some form, presumably earlier, of the book of Deuteronomy as we know it.

Q. 70. Would you give me an example of what you mean by deuteronomic style and theology?

This question is a tall order, in that it deserves a very long answer. I would like to break it down into several questions that follow. The style or language of Deuteronomy is rather immediately apparent if it is compared to the rest of the Pentateuch. There is a characteristic terminology. The famous questions and answers of Micah 6:6–8 have another accent in Deuteronomy 10:12–13: "And now, Israel, what does the Lord, your God ask of you but to fear the Lord your God and to walk in his ways, to love and serve the Lord your God with your whole heart and whole soul, to keep the Lord's commandments and statutes that I enjoin on you today for your good?" One expression is heaped upon another: fear, walk, love, serve, keep. This is typical deuteronomic language. "Fear" is defined by obedience to the ways of God, total service, and love. Fear of the Lord is well described in the account of the Sinai experience in chapter 5: "The Lord our God has shown us his glory and majesty. We have heard the voice from the midst of the fire and have discovered today that we can still live after God has spoken with us…If we hear the voice of the Lord our God again we shall die. For what mortal has heard as we have the voice of the living God speaking from the midst of the fire and still lived?" (5:24–26). God's reaction to this is: "Would that they might always be of such a mind: to fear me and keep my commandments always…" (5:29). There is an intensity in speech that leads to a repetition of words like the pounding of a hammer: "Therefore, keep the commandments of the Lord your God, walking in his ways and fearing him" (8:6; cf. 8:11).

In addition to this unparalleled emphasis on personal involvement, the phrase "statutes and ordinances" occurs frequently, a global designation of the items in the rules and policies described in the code, 12:1–26:15. They are the explication of the covenantal decrees (the Decalogue; cf. 4:44; 5:2; 6:2, 17, etc.). When future generations ask for the meaning of what the Lord has commanded (6:20), a catechetical lesson is read off: "We were the slaves of Pharaoh in Egypt but the Lord brought us out with a mighty hand.…Then he commanded us to keep all these statutes, to fear the Lord our God for our lasting good and life as on this day" (6:21–24).

Q. 71. What are the theological emphases of Deuteronomy?

I don't wish to insinuate that the points raised in the preceding question are not also theological; they surely are, and they are the heart of deuteronomic theology that is praxis and not theory. But one can single out certain theoretical ideas that are behind some of the praxis. (1) The first example is centralization of worship, i.e., that there is to be no worship of the Lord on the high places, but only in Jerusalem, "the place that the Lord your God will choose as a dwelling for his name" (12:11 and many other places). This has been called a "Name" theology, but it is not easy for nominalists like ourselves to grasp its significance. The name is the person; this is a real presence. At the same time, however, the true presence of the Lord is in heaven with the members of the heavenly court. The choice of Jerusalem/Zion did not impair the divine transcendence, but humanly speaking it made for an immanence that was dear to the Deuteronomists. Moreover, it was a very practical move, since it was likewise aimed at the high places where the Lord was also worshiped. It should be remembered that the high places and shrines throughout the land, many of them sanctified by the memory of the patriarchs, were not in themselves idolatrous. In 1 Kings 18:30 Elijah repairs an altar of the Lord that had been thrown down, and there he offers sacrifice to the Lord in competition with the prophets of Baal. At that time (middle of the ninth century) there was no centralization. But it was precisely the danger of the "baalization" of the Lord and due worship that was the problem; *yhwh* was not to be associated with Baal worship. This mandate of centralization is another tie-in with the so-called deuteronomic history. The judgment that is passed on the kings is on the basis of whether they tolerated the high places. And the judgment is retroactive; the criterion of Deuteronomy is applied to previous generations. The "sin of Jeroboam" (Jeroboam 1, who after the split of the united kingdom established sacrificial altars at Dan and Bethel) cast a long shadow over the kings of northern Israel. It made no *difference* that the "calves" were probably originally conceived as thrones for the divinity; they could easily be taken as images, and therefore worthy of deuteronomic ire.

(2) Another central idea of deuteronomic theology is that of retribution. Obedience or loyalty to the God of the covenant and his wishes guarantees long life in the land, and this motive is used very many times (e.g., 4:40). By the same token, disobedience and sinfulness will merit punishment of the most dire kind (4:26). The blessings and curses of chapter 28 are another illustration. In many parts of the Bible we are reminded of the power of both blessing (Isaac and Jacob) and curse (Ps 109). More than words are involved; it is the power behind the words to affect the individual. Chapter 28 holds out the retribution in terms of the land and life:

> Blessed be you in the city,
>   and blessed in the country;
> Blessed be the fruit of your womb,
>   the products of your soil, and the fruit of your livestock,
>   the increase of your herd and the issue of your flock,

Blessed be your basket and your kneading bowl;
Blessed be you in your coming in,
    and blessed in your going out! (28:3–6)

The curse corresponding to this blessing negates it exactly, "Cursed be you..." (28:16–19).

The particular blessings/cursings in this chapter belong to a rite celebrated by the people as part of covenant celebration and find a counterpart in the oaths sworn by subject vassals to sovereigns in the ancient Near East (see Q. 73). One might ask if this view of divine justice can stand. First of all, it is to be understood on a collective, not on an individual level. On an individual level, such as the case of Job, the problem of divine justice becomes acute since Job has done nothing wrong. On the collective level it did not escape questioning; this is illustrated by the saying about the fathers eating the grapes and the children's teeth being on edge (Jer 31:29; Ez 18:2). Indeed, Ezekiel calls for individual responsibility and not global condemnation. Once more, as so often in the Bible, we are confronted by tensions in the understanding of God—and there is no simple solution to the mysterious divine ways. One should also recall the tendency of human beings in advocating their viewpoints, however correct these may be as generalizations. The deuteronomists had a rigid view of divine justice. It was orthodox and "safe," but ultimately it could not explain everything. For their immediate purposes, it provided some explanation of the colossal calamity brought about by the destruction of Jerusalem and the exile.

Q. 72. Why is there such an emphasis throughout Deuteronomy on the present moment, the "today"?

You have caught out one of the characteristic words in the book. By and large it indicates the present moment that is seen to be the time for choice, for deciding in the present what the future will be like. The striking statement of Moses in Deuteronomy 5:2–3 illustrates an unusual quality of the deuteronomic today: "The Lord our God made a covenant with us at Horeb. Not with our fathers did the Lord make this covenant, but with us, all of us who are alive here today." Well, with whom was the Horeb (i.e., Sinai) covenant made? Obviously it was made with the generation of Israelites who in the present context had already died in the desert. But this is denied; the covenant has been made with the Israelites whom Moses is addressing: "The Lord spoke with you face to face on the mountain from out of the fire" (v. 4). Time is wiped out: today is also forty years ago, and what happened then happens today. This is the language of covenant renewal that permeates the book. As we shall see there are two covenants that play a role in this work: the Sinai covenant, and the Moab covenant (cf. Dt 29:9–14).

Q. 73. Hasn't it been shown that the covenant idea in Israel was taken over from treaty forms that existed in the ancient Near East?

That is not so; the idea of the covenant is not derived from treaty forms. Rather, the proper question is this: Did the treaty forms influence the recording of the covenant in Israel's tradition? The way in which the covenant is described in Deuteronomy would be an example of such influence. The positions on this question have varied considerably over the last forty years since the similarity between the Israelite covenant and the treaties was first remarked. Some argue that the covenant idea was taken over from the secular treaties and is thus the basis of Israel's relationship to the Lord. That is one extreme, and unlikely. Others argue that specifically Deuteronomy was the fruit of editing previous materials by court scribes who were aware of the foreign treaties and followed their pattern in the structuring of Israel's relationship to the Lord (cf. M. Weinfeld, *Deuteronomy 1–11* [New York: Doubleday, 1991] 9–11, 62–65). It should be emphasized that there are various kinds of treaties that have been discovered in the ancient world, and these range from Hittite treaties in the second millennium to the Assyrian treaties of the first millennium. The most pertinent is the so-called suzerainty treaty in which a sovereign king enters into a political relationship with a vassal state. The covenant formulary, as it is called, includes the following key elements: historical prologue, statement of allegiance, stipulations, list of (divine) witnesses, curses and blessings, and a deposition of the agreement. These can be correlated with the historical prologue in Deuteronomy 1–4, the oath of allegiance in Deuteronomy 6:4ff., the stipulations or obligations of the vassal in Deuteronomy 12–26, the blessings and curses in Deuteronomy 27–28, and the deposit of the document in Deuteronomy 31:24–26. This correlation does not mean that

Deuteronomy is a covenant formulary; the biblical work is clearly patterned on the speeches of Moses, but one can catch echoes of the suzerainty treaties of the Fertile Crescent. I would prefer a cautious answer to the question, and to speak of influence that the knowledge of secular treaties could have had on the formulation of the Israelite covenant. The final word on this has not yet been written.

Q. 74. I am confused by all this covenant talk; how many covenants do we have in the Bible?

In earlier answers (QQ. 13, 31), we have spoken about the covenant with Abraham and the Sinai covenant. You will recall that there was a significant *difference* between the two: the first was promissory—the Lord made the promise, without laying obligations upon Abraham. In contrast, the Sinai covenant was an agreement in which Israel undertook to live up to requirements imposed by the Lord. Thus we read in Exodus 19:5–8: "If you hearken to my voice and keep my covenant, you shall be my special possession out of all the peoples....The people all answered together: 'Everything the Lord has spoken, we will do....'"

Now in the book of Deuteronomy we are dealing with a second covenant made in Moab. This, too, is a covenant of obligation for Israel, as the tenor of Moses' speeches and the inclusion of the Decalogue and the laws of chapters 12–26 make clear. The distinction from the Sinai covenant is explicit in 28:69 (29:1): "These are the words of the covenant that the Lord commanded Moses to make with the Israelites in the land of Moab, in addition to the covenant that he made with them at Horeb." At Horeb (Sinai) God told Moses everything, even down to the minute liturgical details of the priestly writings that are swept into the narrative (Exodus 19 to Numbers 10, we recall, is one continuous narrative). Quite differently, at Moab Moses tells the people everything by means of his discourses. From Deuteronomy 5:27–31 we learn that the people request Moses to "tell us what the Lord our God tells you." The Lord gives to Moses all the stipulations that the people are to observe. Thus, there are two deliveries of the one basic obligatory relationship in which Israel stands vis-à-vis the Lord. But there are not really two *different* covenants: Moab affirms Sinai.

One might even say that the Moabite covenant is more of a covenant renewal, but it is a renewal that has learned the lesson of Israel's unfaithful history as a people since the days of Moses, and now the opportunity to stand together and affirm loyalty to the Lord of the covenant is offered. This is suggested by Deuteronomy 31:9–13, where Moses orders that "the book of the law" (Deuteronomy? see Q. 69) be read aloud every seven years. In Deuteronomy 31:24–27 he is described as writing out the words of the whole law, and having the scroll put inside the Ark of the Covenant where it will be available for the instruction of future generations and also as a witness to Israel's own infidelity. Unfortunately we have practically no concrete information about covenant renewal (but see Joshua 24), i.e., just how it was carried out. The urgency which Deuteronomy imposes on the audience to make a choice, and the clarity with which the fruits of the choice are described, suggest the atmosphere of covenant renewal: "Here, then, I have today set before you life and prosperity, death and doom....I call heaven and earth today to witness against you: I have set before you life and death, the blessing and the curse. Choose life..." (*NAB* Dt 30:15–19). The repetition of the moment, "today," has already been singled out in Q. 72, and it is another call for decision.

Q. 75. Will you describe the various levels at which the book of Deuteronomy can be read and applied?

We might call the first the "wilderness" level. By that I mean we put ourselves in the shoes of the Israelites who have survived, the new community sired by the lost generation that never got out of the desert. This is the basic group that is addressed. The lessons of the sorry past are read out, and they are challenged to enter into the future that God intended for them. But this generation never did hear the speeches of Moses. The first to learn of the deuteronomic tradition would have been the Israelites of the centuries preceding the discovery of the "deuteronomic" book of the law in the reign of Josiah (see Q. 69). We have no clear idea of the way this tradition was described to them.

The second level could be described as the Josianic level, because of Josiah's penitent reaction upon hearing the book of the law identified and read out to him (2 Kings 22:11–13). It was enough to spearhead his ill-fated reform that never fulfilled its promise. The failure of such a powerful prophet as Jeremiah (e.g., see his appeals to the people in Jeremiah 7 and 26) would indicate that the choice was death, not life.

The third level would be the exilic/post-exilic audience that read (or heard read) Deuteronomy more or less in the form in which we have it today. The refugees from exile could understand their tragic history, but they could also profit from the encouragement to choose life after the near-death in Babylon. Indeed some passages clearly have the exile in mind, e.g., Deuteronomy 30:1–10, in which there is the promise to bring back those who have been scattered among the nations. Deuteronomy could be heard as an explanation of the past, but also as a harbinger of a better future.

A fourth level can also be discerned: the modern reader who identifies with the people of God in its weakness, in its potential, in its future. We can individualize the appeals of Moses, hearing them as addressed to ourselves as well as to ancient Israel. Deuteronomy is a document of renewal (cf. R.E. Murphy in *Concilium* 89 [1973] 26–36), and the call for a decision is almost a daily occurrence in our lives. We are addressed by the *Shema*—"hear" (O Israel).

Q. 76. What is this "Shema" that you have just mentioned?

This is the first word of Deuteronomy 6:4 and it means "Listen!" The command is frequent in the book (cf. 5:1; 9:1; 20:3; 27:9). It is a strong word that carries also the notion: hear and obey. In the wisdom literature, hearing is not passive, but active, meaning: Obey! (Prov 1:8). The term is really another example of the intensity of the deuteronomic language. Unfortunately the translation of 6:4 is not agreed upon by all, as a perusal of various versions will show. The differences come more from the ambiguities of the text and the context (see S. D. McBride, *Interpretation* 27 [1973] 273–306, especially 292–93). The statement is an answer to "Who is our God?" Then it can be rendered: "Our God is the Lord, the Lord alone." McBride translated the whole Shema (6:4–5) as follows:

> Hear, O Israel!
>   Our God is Yahweh, Yahweh alone!
> And love Yahweh your God with all your heart,
>   with all your life, indeed with all your capacity!

This command is part of the daily prayer (said twice daily) of a Jewish person. It has been supplemented over the years with other passages (e.g., Dt 6:7–9; 11:13–21; Num 15:37–41). Its theological emphasis is clearly monotheistic, but it has also served as an emphatic expression of the unity of the one God of Israel.

In Christian theology verse 5 has received more attention, as the "Great Commandment." In Matthew 22:38 Jesus calls this the greatest and first commandment, and adds a "second" from Leviticus 19:18, to love the neighbor as oneself. This is, of course, a basic text for Christian faith.

Q. 77. Why are the Ten Commandments given twice (Exodus 20; Deuteronomy 5)?

Because the Decalogue is very suitable, even necessary, in both books. In Exodus it is the basis of the new relationship that is to exist between the Lord and Israel: what kind of a God is the Lord and what is expected of a people that is to be elect or chosen. There are some differences between the two versions, but the obligations do not change. Since Deuteronomy presents the covenant made in Moab, this fundamental law needs to be stated again, this time with some characteristically deuteronomic flourishes. The first commandment is in Deuteronomy 5:6–10. It identifies the Lord as the leader of the exodus who alone deserves Israel's worship—"no other gods besides me." It has often been noted that the existence of other gods is taken for granted, but they are to be disregarded. This is henotheism or monolatry that is on its way to become eventually a more theoretical monotheism.

Somewhat neglected by us is the accompanying prohibition concerning images. There are to be no images of *yhwh*. It is not merely that Israelites should not make and serve images of other gods (a common practice in the ancient Near East), but the Lord is imageless; only human beings are an image of the Lord (Gen 1:26–27). The reasoning behind this prohibition is not obvious. It is said that images of a deity enabled human beings to exercise some control by means of the image; the deity was, as it were, localized, boxed in. But this sounds more like modern reasoning. The command certainly opposes a facile understanding of the anthropomorphic descriptions of the Lord in the Old Testament. God is said to have eyes and ears, etc., but no image of this God is to be made! There is a marvelous tension between anthropomorphic imagery and the imagelessness of the Lord.

The "jealousy" of God also needs to be understood correctly. Moderns tend to consider jealousy as a weakness, an uncertainty in one's love and trust toward another. The Hebrew word also connotes zeal, passion and ardor, and these aspects are uppermost in the customary phrase, a "jealous" God who will not tolerate infidelity in the people. Once again (Dt 5:9–10) we are confronted with the collective dimension of the divine treatment of the just and the unjust; cf. Exodus 34:6–7; Numbers 14:18. The divine mercy outruns the divine wrath (cf. Dt 7:9–10, where the personal retribution of the sinner is mentioned).

The sabbath observance is unique to Israel. The Exodus tradition associated the rest with the seventh day of creation, when God "rested" from the six days of work. The obligation of rest remains; in that way the day is "hallowed," as is explicitly stated in Exodus 20:11. There is no broad definition of what work, or failure to observe the rest, might be. In Exodus 35:3 there is an explicit injunction against kindling fire on this day. In Deuteronomy an additional motive is given for the sabbath observance: the former slaves are to remember their former status, and how the Lord freed them from Egypt.

It is obvious that Christianity, with few exceptions, has substituted Sunday for Saturday sabbath. And the reason of course is the celebration (of the day) of the resurrection. For centuries there was also an observance of rest on this day, an abstention from "servile work," as it was called. In the secularized civilization in which we now live, this kind of rest seems to have practically disappeared, and while the day may be marked by religious service in the morning (at least where the time is not usurped by golf), the rest of the day is too often spent in ways that are simply distracting from serious thought about God (TV and football, anyone?).

In the case of Israel, the sabbath became a basic expression of faith, "a sign forever between me and the people of Israel" to be kept as "a perpetual covenant" (Ex 31:16–17). Unfortunately this has not registered in the Christian psyche.

Finally it is important to distinguish between revelation and inspiration here. For the most part, the prohibitions in the Decalogue can be replicated in ancient Near Eastern culture. They are not specific revelations, but mostly drawn from the prevailing ethos.

Q. 78. I have heard of workers taking a "sabbatical" from their labors. Is this connected with sabbath observance?

Strictly speaking this has nothing to do with the sabbath observance. But it is patterned after another biblical practice in which "sabbath," or rest, plays a role. According to Exodus 23:10–11 and Leviticus 25:1–7 the land that was being farmed was to lie fallow every seventh year. This was a rest for the land, which really belonged to God, and not to the individual. If anything grew up during that period it was to be left for the poor and the beasts of the field (Ex 23:11). This applied also to vineyards and olive groves. This was a "sabbath for the Lord." But Deuteronomy goes further than this. Every seventh year there is to be a remission of debts (the Hebrew *shemitta*). This applied only to members of the community, not to foreigners. This law may have been somewhat utopian, to judge from what we know of Israelite history, but there is a marvelous serenity in Deuteronomy 15:4, "No one among you will be in need, for the Lord will surely bless you in the land that the Lord your God is giving you to occupy as your heritage." The writings of the prophets prove that this often remained only an ideal. Verses 6–11 strictly command sharing with those in need, and it attempts to forestall the devious practice of holding back because the year of remission was approaching— "or he [the debtor] will cry out to the Lord, and you shall be held guilty" (v. 9). At the same time Deuteronomy is realistic. The poor, it says, will never disappear from the land (v. 11), but this is no excuse; one's hand is to be always open to them. The same generosity was to be shown toward Hebrew slaves. They were to be freed in the seventh year, and they were not to be dismissed empty-handed, but rather with a proportion of the blessings (from flocks, threshing floor and wine press) that the owner had received from God. The prophet Jeremiah condemns king Zedekiah for manipulating the law of release and failing to observe it (Jer 34:13–17); hence the Lord will "release" Israel to the sword, pestilence and famine.

It is obvious how distant from the biblical ideal is our modern "sabbatical."

Q. 79. How does Deuteronomy view the levites?

Levites are viewed as priests, and the phrase "levitical priests" is common. Who were they? Recall the centralization of worship (in one place, and eventually in Jerusalem) that the deuteronomic reform was trying to achieve. What would be the fate of those who served at the many shrines throughout the land? They were now out of their former employment since sacrifice was to be restricted to Jerusalem.

Since levites had no share in the land, they had to live on charity, portions of the sacrifices made to the Lord (Dt 18:3–5). Deuteronomy sees their functions as "to minister in the name of the Lord" (18:5), giving judgment (17:9) and instruction in the law. In the post-exilic period they are seen as aids to the clergy, but with exalted roles (Num 18:21–24). Their glory is that they received no special allotment of land; the Lord was their inheritance, and hence they depended on the charity of their brethren.

Q. 80. What is the meaning of Moses' claim that the Lord will raise up a prophet like him (Dt 18:15)?

This famous line occurs in the context of a strong prohibition of the "abominations" in Canaan, where contact with the other world was sought by child sacrifice, fortune-telling, soothsaying, diviners, and necromancy. All such means of communication are outlawed. Instead, the line of prophets that we know from the Bible (both those who wrote and those who did not write, e.g., Elijah, Elisha) are promised—they are prophets like Moses. In 18:17 this is traced back to a decision of the Lord at Sinai: "I will put my words into his mouth"—the essence of prophetism—and there is a serious obligation to hear and obey. However, there is also the recognition that a prophet can go it on his own, or even speak in the name of other gods (18:20). The test lies in the fulfillment or non-fulfillment of the oracle proffered by such a prophet. However, the reality was not all that simple. In Deuteronomy it is recognized that a prophet can urge the people along the way of untruth, even to follow other gods. Even if the sign or wonder that he foretells should come to pass, he is to be put to death; it is the Lord testing Israel to see if it loves him with all its heart and soul!

These theoretical reactions to those who have come to be called "false" prophets were not all that easy to put into practice. One is reminded of the altercation between Jeremiah and the prophet Hananiah in Jeremiah 28. Hananiah simply contradicts the message of Jeremiah, stating in effect that yoke of the king of Babylon shall be broken and Israel freed from the threat of disaster. Jeremiah applies the criterion: it is when the word of the prophet is verified that one knows he truly speaks for God. With great flair Hananiah removed the wooden yoke, a symbol, that Jeremiah had across his neck, and broke it. What does Jeremiah do? He walks away. Only later from the Lord does he receive the message to let Hananiah know that the yoke of wood will be replaced by an iron yoke, the rule of Babylon when Jerusalem is destroyed. The essential point here is that there was no easy criterion available. Jeremiah could well have had doubts about himself. Was he hearing the Lord correctly? Was Hananiah speaking the truth (the "truth" that the whole population of Jerusalem wanted to hear)? Jeremiah had to retreat until he was satisfied that he understood what the Lord was saying through him. And the people, how were they to judge? If one reads the prophets, one gets the impression that practically the real criterion was the obvious holiness and integrity of the prophet. Some were convinced by it; others were not. Or if they were convinced by it, they refused to abide by what the prophet said (e.g., King Zedekiah and Jeremiah; cf. Jer 38:14–28).

Deuteronomy 18:15 came to be interpreted in an eschatological fashion—a prophet like Moses was to return in the end-time, and we see the application of it to Jesus in John 1:21 and 6:14; cf. Acts 3:22–23.

Q. 81. How was justice administered in Israel?

This question deserves to be raised because of the several methods that were adopted over the course of Israel's history. Perhaps the oldest, or at least the most simple, was the administration of justice at "the city gates," so often mentioned in the Bible (e.g., Am 5:10, 12, 15). Here the elders of the town would render a verdict. A vivid scene is described in Ruth 4:1–12, and a criminal case, in this instance a subversion of justice due to lying witnesses, is found in 1 Kings 21, where Naboth is stoned to death. A more official structure is that of judges, probably appointed by royal authority, that is mentioned in Deuteronomy 16:18–20. These officials are warned against bribery. For "a bribe blinds the eyes even of the wise and twists the pleas of the just." Attached to the admonition to be just is the great promise of this book: "that you may have life and possess the land that the Lord your God is giving you." There is even the recognition of a need for a higher court. In such cases one went to Jerusalem (Dt 17:9, "the place the Lord your God has chosen"), where priests and secular judges have been appointed for adjudication. One of the most unusual judicial settlements is specified in Deuteronomy 21:1–9. In the case of an unknown murderer, a measurement of the distance from the corpse to the nearest town is to be taken. The elders of that town then assume responsibility and take a young heifer down to a flowing wadi. They cut the throat of the animal and wash their hands over the heifer as they pray to the Lord to remove from the midst of the people the guilt of shedding innocent blood.

Deuteronomy also provides for cities of refuge in the land of Canaan (19:1–7), as well as the three appointed in Transjordan (4:41–43). In this case the places were no real sanctuaries, due to the deuteronomic centralization of worship in Jerusalem. The motivation behind this institution was to prevent blood vengeance, which was exacted even in accidental killing. Deuteronomy gives the example of an unintentional homicide due to a flying axe-head. On the other hand a murderer who flees to a city of refuge is to be apprehended by the elders of his native town and given over to the *go'el*, or avenger of blood, to be put to death. Numbers 35:33–34 has enunciated the principle behind this: bloodshed pollutes the land and the only atonement for this is the blood of the one who shed it. There should be no defilement of the land "in the midst of which I dwell; for I am the Lord who dwells in the midst of the Israelites" (35:34).

One may not leave this issue of murder and vengeance without at least recalling the incident of David and Uriah, the husband of Bathsheba. It was also true that the king of Israel was a minister of justice; indeed Absalom, the son of David, raises a claim that David is not expediting justice at the court (2 Sam 15:2–4). But who was to judge the king? In the incident of the murder of Uriah, we have the "case" that Nathan brings before David: the marvelous parable about the rich man and the poor man and his one treasure, the little ewe lamb. David's anger is aroused by the story and he cries out that such a person who deprives the poor man deserves to die. And Nathan's stunning reply is, "You are the man!" David has really passed judgment upon himself and his adulterous union, followed by the death of Uriah. He was trapped by his reaction to the indirectness of the prophet.

Q. 82. Was the king an "absolute monarch" in Israel?

Some acted that way, and in the case of several we have vivid scenes of opposition of prophets to kings (one thinks of Elijah and his opposition to Ahab, or of Zedekiah and Jeremiah). The king was the anointed of God, but the example of the bravery of the prophets in confronting royalty is without example in the Fertile Crescent. It is striking that Deuteronomy pays so little attention to kingship. This is to be expected perhaps from a document that seems to have had its origins in the north where there was no oracle about the perdurance of the royal line as in the case of David (2 Sam 7). Instead, the king is discussed only briefly (Dt 17:14–20), and in a critical way. It seems as though the unhappy example of Solomon was in the mind of the writer. The king is not to have a great number of wives, nor accumulate silver and gold or a great number of horses, nor do any horse-trading with Egypt. The typical deuteronomic influence comes in vv. 18–19. The king is to have "a copy of this law" for constant reading, and is expected to fulfill the words of the law. In other words, he is expected to be like any other Israelite, totally devoted to the Lord.

This brief mention of kingship is to be expected from the generally unfortunate history of royalty in both kingdoms. At the same time, it proves surprising to many readers in view of the great attention given to kingship in the historical and prophetical books of the Bible. It amounts to a put-down of royalty, or at least putting it in its place.

Q. 83. How serious was the law of tithing in the Old Testament?

In general, tithing means giving up a tenth (tithe) of one's annual income for religious purposes. However, there seems also to have been a royal tithe, or, better, tax. This was collected by the king, as may be inferred from 1 Samuel 8:15–17. The specific laws governing the practice of tithing changed at various times and in various places. Deuteronomy organizes it in the light of centralization of worship.

Tithes were to be brought to the central sanctuary (Jerusalem) on the occasion of the pilgrim feasts of Passover, Weeks and Tabernacles. However, Deuteronomy recognized the possibility that the pilgrimage could not be made in view of the distance from Jerusalem. So the land tithe could be exchanged for money. The money could also be exchanged for food at the temple. Specific legislation is given for levites. Every third year tithes are to be shared with levites, the alien, and the poor such as orphans and widows (cf. Dt 26:12–15 and 14:28–29).

The deuteronomic code closes in chapter 26 with the touching ceremony of the offering of the first fruits in Jerusalem. These are put in a basket and set before the Lord with the beautiful prayer: "Today I acknowledge to the Lord my God that I have indeed come into the land that he swore to our fathers to give us." There follows a succinct summary of the deliverance from Egypt (from Jacob to Moses) and a joyous meal with levites and aliens, along with the family. Deuteronomy never allows its readers to forget the *gift of the land*. There was one God, one land and one worship in that land at Jerusalem. The land was lost in the exile, but it was returned, and the deuteronomic emphasis on the land is both nostalgic (on the lips of Moses speaking to those who are to possess the land) and hopeful (as read by the exiles who had returned to the land).

Q. 84. Wasn't the deuteronomic view of war ruthless and inhumane?

Your question is concerned with what is called the holy war, in which the opponents are "doomed," or put under the "ban" (Hebrew *cherem*). The first mention of this total war is in Deuteronomy 2:32–34 when Israel conquers Sihon: "We took all his cities, and we doomed all of them (men, women and children) and there were no survivors." The same treatment is meted out to Og of Bashan (3:4). It is explicitly noted that the material possessions, the booty, are appropriated by the Israelites. This was not in line with the rules of the "doom" war, at least as practiced against Canaanites (see the case of Achan in Joshua 7:1, 16). The "theory" of total war, as it may be called, is contained especially in Deuteronomy 20. Primary is the assurance that the Lord will be with the Israelites against any odds, and they are assured of this by a kind of war discourse that was to be delivered by the priest (vv. 2–4). Exceptions are made: exempt are those who have built new houses but not yet settled in them, or planted a young vineyard and have not yet enjoyed its fruits, or the newly betrothed. In going to war one should sue for peace, but if there is no agreement, the Lord will deliver victory to Israel: males are to be slain, and women, children, livestock and booty belong to the victors. But now a distinction is made. The previous rules obtain for cities that are distant, but in the case of those that are occupied by Canaanites, not one is to be left alive. This is particularly clear from Deuteronomy 7:1–4 where the seven typical "enemies" in the promised land are mentioned by name. The reason given for this total extermination is that these peoples would tempt the Israelites to serve other gods.

What is to be said about this martial spirit? Did the Lord *order* this kind of slaughter? No, it is Israel's interpretation, the deuteronomic interpretation, of the divine will. One can point to the fact that such violent wars were part of the culture of the day (e.g., Moab practices the ban for its god, Chemosh). But this does not really touch on the responsibility, which is human and not divine. Secondly, are the accounts of such wholesale slaughter dependable? If one reads Deuteronomy 7 carefully, it is apparent from 7:3 that the Canaanites survived the ban, because there is legislation against intermarriage with them. Hence one may conclude that the doom war was more theory than reality. It may have arisen from vows made by warriors and then seen as an obligation that they had to fulfill by living up to the terms they had set. When one looks at the record of the conquest, one is inclined to question the sweeping claims made for the wars against the inhabitants of Canaan. Why would the deuteronomic school of writers, then, be so adamant about this type of war? Because they recognized the apostasy of the people throughout their history as associated with the idolatry that the Canaanites practiced. At least in their ideology they could urge fidelity upon the people in the light of the past victories the Lord had won for Israel. One should recall the impact this would make upon exilic readers of the deuteronomic tradition; the past was idealized. Furthermore, there was no practical danger from war in the post-exilic period. Nonetheless, one cannot gainsay the fact that Israel understood its Lord as one who would not hesitate to carry on this type of war. Today we can only recognize this as a limitation on the revelation given to Israel.

Divine approval of this sort is not to be sought in our day, and if nothing else the crusades, with the motto "God wills it," are an example from which Christians should learn. It is incumbent upon moderns to realize that war is barbaric in every age, and that Israel was no more barbaric than its neighbors or than modern armies. It is easier to wipe out whole populations by pressing a button, with our modern efficiency, but this is no less barbaric. People who are offended by the doom war or by Psalm 137 need to recall the practices of their own civilization.

Q. 85. How did the knowledge of having been "chosen" affect Israel?

There can be no denying that this was a privilege. The words of Exodus 19:4–6 portray Israel as being the special possession of the Lord, and it is to be a holy people. But on its part, it must show that it is obedient and faithful to the covenant. The love relationship must be reciprocal. These ideas are repeated in Deuteronomy 7 where Israel is said to be *chosen*. More than once Israel is reminded that it was out of pure love that it was chosen (4:37; 7:8; 10:15; 23:6), either out of love for the fathers (patriarchs) and fidelity to the promises made to them, or simply because of the mysterious divine love. This note of love appears as well in Hosea (e.g., 11:1–4) and Jeremiah (e.g., 31:2). Certainly the choice was not due to Israel's greatness and size among the nations, "for you are really the smallest of all nations" (Dt 7:7). There is a real poignancy in the way Deuteronomy describes an imagined reaction of the nations in 4:6–8. When peoples see the wisdom and intelligence that is manifest in the Torah, they will proclaim: "This great nation is truly a wise and intelligent people." Moses is speaking, and he goes on to say that no other nation has a divinity as close to it as the Lord. Hearing this, the exiles could only be conscience-stricken at the failure to have lived faithfully. The prophets knew how to use the election of the people in such a way as to prevent hubris. Amos proclaims, "You alone have I known of all the families of the earth! Therefore I will punish you..." (3:2). Election was for service; it brought obligation, not empty status. Israel had to remain faithful.

This love relationship might seem at first to be a simple *quid pro quo*, namely, that it was to Israel's benefit to be loyal to the Lord—or else! This is the perspective that Satan took in the judgment of Job (Job 1:9): "Is it for nothing that Job is God-fearing?" There is always the temptation to be "good" for ignoble reasons. Job proved worthy of the divine trust. And ultimately so did Israel, as it struggled with its mysterious God.

You might well ask: If Israel is "chosen," what is the situation of the rest of the nations? Deuteronomy had an answer to that. In 32:8–9 it is described this way in the Song of Moses:

> When the Most High assigned the nations their heritage,
>   when he parceled out the descendants of Adam,
> He set up the boundaries of the peoples
>   after the number of the sons of God;
> While the Lord's own portion was Jacob,
>   his hereditary share was Israel (*NAB*).

In this view a decision is made in the assembly of the heavenly court, where the "sons of God" dwell (cf. Ps 29). Each of them receives a nation as a heritage, but Israel is reserved for the Lord. The poem at this point has tamed the myth of the pantheon of gods; they have become patrons of the nations—"guardian angels," if you will. Israel's relationship to the Lord is then developed in the following lines (vv. 10ff.).

Q. 86. What is the "Song of Moses"?

Don't let the word "song" mislead you. It is a long poem, very much as you might find in the book of Psalms, and indeed, it is comparable to Psalm 78. Of course, the psalms are songs, and this Song of Moses was destined for precisely that use. The poem is anticipated in Deuteronomy 31:19 in the command of the Lord that "this song" be written out and taught to the Israelites for their recitation. It is a song that will be a witness for God against them. The whole mood is one of a kind of resigned attitude to Israel's eventual infidelity. After their idolatry and trials they will hear this song that will have been kept alive among them, to their shame. It is recorded that Moses wrote "this song" that same day and taught it to the people (31:22), and that he recited it from beginning to end to them.

The literary form of the poem is not easy to determine. The poet begins with an ornate introduction, calling for the attention of heaven and earth to his invigorating praise of the Lord (at the end there is an inclusion or repetition of the idea of praise; 32:43). The praise of the Lord for the providence that singled out Israel and delivered them from Egypt (who is not mentioned explicitly) quickly turns to an indictment of the ingratitude of the people to their Rock, a term repeated frequently in this song (32:4, 15, 18, 30, 31 and see v. 32). The firm fidelity of God is spurned by the foolish people. In striking rhetorical questions they are reminded of their "father who created you" (6), "the Rock that begot you," "the God who gave you birth" (18). They should remember the traditions of the past that tell of the Lord's care for the infant people. The story begins in the "howling desert" where God spread wings over them and bore them up on pinions. The Lord fed them with great prosperity, such as the "blood of grapes" (wine). But what happened? As Jacob (a frequent name for the entire people) became sated, he spurned his Rock and honored idols, offering sacrifices to "no-gods." At this point the poet introduces the first of the soliloquies of the Lord. God determines to hide his face and provide appropriate punishment: "Since they have provoked me with their 'no-god'…I will provoke them with a 'no-people'" (v. 21). Although some would historicize this as referring to the scourge of the Philistines (cf. 1 Sam 4–6), it may be merely a rhetorical flourish, symbolic of Israel's inconsistency in its relationship with the Lord. The Lord determines to release a furious attack upon Israel, and a litany of woes is described (vv. 22–25). On the verge of extinguishing them, God recalls how their enemies would boast that this was *their* victory, and that the Lord was impotent. But such a "no-people" should realize that victory over Israel would not have been so easy unless the Rock, their Lord, had abandoned them (v. 30). The poet condemns these enemies of Israel, and the Lord begins another soliloquy about the disasters and vengeance that will be visited against them in favor of Israel, and delivers a taunt to those who would put their trust in any "rock" but himself, and makes the majestic proclamation (v. 39):

> See then that I, I am he;
>> there is no God besides me.
> It is I who put to death and make alive.
>> I wound and I heal.
>> No one can rescue from my hand.

One more we are reminded of the all-pervasive activity of the Lord; everything that happens can be traced to divine agency or causality. He swears to take ferocious vengeance upon the adversary. The ending is sudden as the poet calls upon the nation and the heavenly court (v. 43, "gods" or "angels") to praise God.

The post-exilic reader of this poem would be powerfully reminded of the past delinquency of Israel, and at the same time challenged once again to recognize their "Rock" in all integrity. For to *yhwh*, the divine warrior, belongs vengeance, and it will be exacted. The concept of the divine warrior in the Bible is a difficult one to handle. It is a very human and anthropomorphic description of the Lord as the exactor of vengeance. In Israel's culture, wars and battles are interwoven into reality in which the martial activity of the Lord is involved. Still, the question arises: Is this another instance of a biblical limitation of the mystery of divine activity, and destined to fall into disuse? Yet the emphasis was necessary for the post-exilic community; they had no "Rock" on which to rely unless the Lord took up arms for them.

Q. 87. What is meant by Moses' "testament"?

"Testament" is used somewhat loosely. On the one hand, it is the last word of the great leader, and on the other it is addressed not to his family, but to the tribes, considering each one by name. The genre of "testament" reminds one of the words of the aging Isaac (Gen 29), blessing Esau and Jacob—or, even more aptly, the blessing that Jacob gives to his sons (Gen 49). Hence these "last words" are more in the line of blessing, and the one who blesses is presumed to have insight into the future. They are framed by an introduction (vv. 1–5) and ending (vv. 25–29). Verses 1–5 describe the Lord's victorious march with the people from Sinai, the Mosaic legislation (Moses is spoken of in the third person), and the kingship established in Jeshurun (a word of uncertain meaning, translated as "darling" by the Septuagint, and standing for Israel; cf. 32:15). The ending (vv. 26–29) addresses Israel ("Jeshurun"), and praises the Lord who is ever ready to deliver them from their enemies.

The blessings are directed to each of the tribes except Simeon, and they are probably to be dated early, after the tribes had been more or less settled in the promised land. The text is often uncertain and several references are obscure. The blessing on Reuben reflects the fact that this tribe died out early. Judah is assured of divine help (against the encroachment of Philistines?). The description of Levi's privileges is quite full: control of Urim and Thummim (see Q. 58), priestly functions, and the interpretation of the Torah for the people. The blessing of Joseph really refers to his sons, Ephraim and Manasseh, especially to Ephraim who became the strongest tribe in the northern kingdom, and enjoyed prosperity. Zebulun and Issachar lay next to each other in the fertile area of the plain of Esdraelon leading up into Galilee. The blessings go on, covering the rest of the tribes, and they all strike the reader as belonging to a later age, when Israel "counted its blessings."

Q. 88. Did Deuteronomy make any changes in the major Israelite feasts?

You are referring to the three feasts of Passover (with which the feast of unleavened bread was associated), Weeks (Pentecost), and Tabernacles (or Succoth). These are old and perennial feasts that had always been observed at least in a local fashion. Now, with the deuteronomic thrust to centralization of worship, they were to be celebrated in Jerusalem (Dt 16:3, 5–7, 15). this brought about modifications in some details. Passover was less of a family feast, but all three occasions were to include the extended family (not just males): sons and daughters, males and female slaves, levites, aliens, and orphans and widows. The note of joy characterized these feasts in which historical remembrance and the fertility of the land were celebrated.

Q. 89. What is the deuteronomic view of the desert period?

Moses' first discourse deals with the desert period after the departure from Sinai (Dt 1:6). The murmuring and revolts in the desert are passed over until the refusal of the Israelites to follow the advice of Joshua and Caleb to enter the land flowing with milk and honey. Indeed, Moses reminds the people that the Lord had carried them, as one would carry a child, all the way to Kadesh-barnea. The major indictment is their refusal to enter Canaan. But for the rest, the victorious advance of the new generation of Israelites—of course with the protection of the Lord—is described (chaps. 2–3). There is a certain ambivalence about the desert period in Israel's traditions. By and large the Pentateuch emphasizes Israel's infidelity to the Lord. Deuteronomy is as much aware of this as the other books—witness the realistic description of the curses that await them if they fail (Dt 28:15–68). Yet it idealizes Israel and its experience in the desert by stressing the unbounded love of God:

> He found them in a wilderness,
>> a wasteland of howling desert.
> He shielded them and cared for them,
>> guarding them as the apple of his eye.
> As an eagle incites its nestlings forth
>> by hovering over its brood,
> So he spread his wings to receive them
>> and bore them up on his pinions (32:10–11, *NAB*).

At least, one may conclude, the Lord was hopelessly in love with the children of Israel. The same love is described so dramatically in Hosea 11:1–4, 8–9. Indeed, this prophet describes Israel's "response" to the divine love "as in the days of her youth when she came up from the land of Egypt" (Hos 2:17). The Lord speaks to Israel in tender accents in Jeremiah 2:2:

> I remember the devotion of your youth,
>> your love as a bride,
> how you followed me in the wilderness,
>> in a land not sown.

The same idealization appears in Jeremiah 32:1–3, but more emphasis is placed on the Lord's grace: "I will place my law within them, and write it upon their hearts. I will be their God and they shall be my people."

Q. 90. How would you sum up the view of Moses as presented in Deuteronomy?

I will try to do that, but first I would like to remind you in a brief way of all the substantial portions of Exodus to Numbers that deal with him. Recall the contest with the pharaoh and the plagues, the journey to Sinai marked by grumbling on the part of the Israelites, Moses' experiences on the mountain communicating with the Lord and receiving all the legislation (Exodus 25 to Numbers 10), the troubling events of the journey from Sinai that climaxed in the refusal to enter into Canaan, the innumerable intercessions that Moses has with the Lord in favor of the fractious people, the revolts against his authority, and finally the early warning that he would be refused entrance into the promised land. We already know a lot of the tradition about Moses before opening the pages of Deuteronomy.

The fact that Deuteronomy is almost all Moses—his discourses— makes us feel a greater intimacy with him. The noble sentiments of deuteronomic loyalty, expressed with such verve and spirit, are manifest in his speeches. Promises and threats are woven together without discouraging those who listen. There is a sense of urgency that weighs upon speaker and listener. When he is refused entrance into the land to which he has led a rebellious and faithless group, the reader feels the injustice of it and sides with the deuteronomic verdict that the people were to blame ("it was on your account," 4:21). Time after time we see him interceding for the people, remonstrating with the Lord that he cannot fail to fulfill the divine promises. We have already noted the prophetic character of this man—that the Lord would raise up a prophet like him (see Q. 80; Dt 18:15). The final words of the book are a proper epitaph. After noting that Moses died at the age of one hundred and twenty (three times forty) years with clear vision and full vigor, we read: "Since then no prophet like Moses arose in Israel; the Lord knew him face to face. He had no equal in all the signs and wonders that the Lord sent him to perform in Egypt against Pharaoh and all his servants and the whole land, and in the great might and terrifying power that Moses displayed in the sight of all Israel" (34:10–12).

Q. 91. It has been said that Deuteronomy is the "center" or heart of the Old Testament; do you agree with that?

As sympathetic as I am to this book, I would not agree that it is the "center" of the Hebrew Bible. The Bible is too rich and varied to be encapsulated in one book. Many scholars have chosen various parts of the Old Testament as constituting its real heart. For example, some have chosen the idea of the covenant as the center. Or a choice is made of the first two commandments: that Israel is to worship *yhwh* alone, and along with this exclusivity is the prohibition of any images of God (much less of foreign divinities). Others have suggested the rule of God and the communion between God and humans, or the statement, "I am *yhwh* your God." These are all helpful insights, but they do not suffice to present the "center," and no consensus has been reached. As a kind of desperate solution, "God" has been proposed, but this is too broad an answer to be helpful.

The attempt to find a center to the Old Testament (and to the New Testament as well, e.g., the doctrine of justification) seems doomed to failure. It is necessarily selective and says more about the theological bias of the one who proclaims the "center." The process is analogous to the establishment of a "canon within the canon." In the latter case one sees the rest of the canon from a limited point. Thus, the letters to the Romans and Galatians can form a canon (within the canon) through which one filters the rest of the biblical message. This is short-sighted. Instead, one should recognize the tensions that exist within the inspired word, and refuse to homogenize the whole. When one considers that the Bible was written over several centuries, and that it records the revelation of a mysterious God, can one truly expect to capture all this in one book or concept?

This does not deny that all of us have favorites within the canonical books of the Bible, books that we read more often than others, or books that we read for specific reasons (hope, encouragement, prayer, etc.). Such a practice does not bring about a narrow view of the Bible, nor does it prevent one from reading broadly across the biblical literature. Our confrontation with various books helps to raise new questions and achieve new insights.

TORAH AND NEW TESTAMENT

Q. 92. What is your view of the relationship between the Testaments?

That is a very large question and it is difficult to answer it briefly. But it has to be faced, for it serves as background to the topic of the Torah and the New Testament, or Judaism and Christianity. I have just used four words that will have to be clearly understood. By Torah I mean the Pentateuch, and by New Testament all the canonical books. By Judaism I mean the dominant rabbinic or Pharisaic Judaism, the teaching of which is contained in the Talmud, the embodiment of the "oral torah," and by Christianity I mean the teaching of the Catholic Church, since that is the group I know best and can write about.

The most general word for the relationship, from a Christian point of view, is that the New Testament "fulfills" the Old Testament. The word "fulfill" or "complete" calls for explanation. I do not have in mind a mechanical correspondence between the Testaments, as if the Old Testament writer was predicting a specific item in the New Testament as the "fulfillment." We know that the Old Testament authors wrote about the future, a glorious future, that the Lord had in store for the chosen people, but they had no blueprint laid out. The New Testament transcends the vision of the Israelite writers, extends it, completes it. This is a matter of Christian faith. It is not settled by exegesis of an Old Testament text that simply yields a New Testament meaning in direct fashion. Christians *believe* that Jesus is the Messiah, just as they believe that he is God. They do not read the Old Testament to *prove* that he is Messiah and the fulfillment of the Old Testament hopes.

From what I have just said it is clear that behind the question of the relationship of two groups of writings (i.e., the Testaments) to each other is Jesus Christ, his identity and mission. It was Christ that had to be understood and explained to the first and succeeding generations of Christians, and these, both Jewish and Gentile, had recourse to the only Bible they knew, *the* Testament in its Hebrew and/or Greek (Septuagint) form in order to understand Jesus the Jew. In reading this Testament, they shared in the current approaches to it; their "hermeneutics" was not a special kind of literary insight, but it may be said that for them Christ was the key and they interpreted his words as indicating fulfillment. The earliest Christian hermeneutic favored the typological approach—itself no stranger to the Hebrew Bible when we read of the typological use of the exodus event in Isaiah 40–55. Hence many persons, things and events in the Old Testament were seen as "types" of Christ or of Christian realities. While not denying the appropriateness of this approach, one may say that it is not popular today. For one thing it was overdone by patristic and medieval writers and it has lost its appeal for most modern readers who prefer a more direct interpretation of the text.

Does this mean that Christian interpretation is tied into a theory of *sensus plenior*, or "fuller sense"? I would prefer to say that the Christian view finds a fuller meaning in the Old Testament text in the light of later revelation. No text is locked into the perspective of the writer. It lives beyond the author and becomes subject to an extension of meaning. This is not unusual; all literary texts live under a future as well as a present meaning, as is indicated also in the use of biblical texts by Jesus and the New Testament writers. Here is not the place to enter into the sticky question of the precise words of Jesus, and how they are to be distinguished from the interpretation given to him and his message by the community, and also from the interpretation afforded by a particular evangelist. Suppose I bring this consideration to an end with the fairly sharp, clear but divisive statement in John 1:17: "The Torah was given through Moses; grace and truth came through Jesus Christ." This does not mean there was no grace and truth in the Torah mediated by Moses, but it does underscore the riches that I meant with the term "fulfillment."

Q. 93. Does "fulfillment" mean the same things as supersession— that the Jewish religion is superseded or is without value in the eyes of God—a kind of "second best"? Don't the words "old" and "new" (covenant/testament) imply this?

Let me address your second question first. The terms "new" and "old" are in a sense conventional and have been bequeathed to us by biblical tradition. Thus, "new" goes back to Jeremiah 31:31–34. This passage was interpreted by the people (probably Essenes) of Qumran who understood themselves as belonging to this new covenant. The Christians of the New Testament also referred this passage to themselves (Heb 8:8–12; 10:16–17). The passage itself is open to ever broadening perspectives. If Jeremiah had in mind the restoration of the people after the exile, he is speaking of one covenant (cf. 31:35–37). The covenant was broken, it is true, but not destroyed. A new covenant is open to God's eschatological plans for the future (indicated also by such statements as Isaiah 2:2–3, that the nations shall go up to the mountain of the Lord—out of Zion shall come forth Torah, the word of the Lord from Jerusalem). So the concept of a "new" (covenant/testament) is contained in the words (e.g., Jeremiah 31) of the "old." I think that one can continue to use the words "New" and "Old" in terms of temporal succession; one is earlier and the other is later. This is not an

evaluation of the validity of either one. Some people prefer to speak of
First/Second Testament when referring to the Bible (since even
"Hebrew Bible" is not a complete expression—parts are written in
Aramaic). There is no easy solution to the propriety of the language
since the question of the canon enters into the discussion: the deutero-
canonical books (Judith, Maccabees, etc.) are not in the First Testament or in the Hebrew/Aramaic Bible. Hence, to answer your second
question: "New" and "Old" refer to temporal succession, and do not
necessarily connote a religious evaluation. The use of the words
covenant/testament are not fraught with the same finality as Old/New.
We understand covenant as the agreement God made with the chosen
people: You shall be my people and I shall be your God. We understand testament (*diatheke*) to mean the written record found in the
entire Bible. Testament rests upon and describes the bond of covenant.

Now for the first question. I would deny that fulfillment and
supersession mean the same thing. They belong to different orders of
judgment. Fulfillment of itself does not invalidate what it fulfills.
Supersession replaces and invalidates what it supersedes. This is not
simply playing with words. Supersessionism eliminates the Old
Testament religion and the Judaism that grew out of it, and I think this
is theologically wrong. I think that the statement of John Paul II in
1980 before official Jewish representatives in Mainz is in agreement
with this point of view. The full text can be found in *Origins* 10 (1980)
#25, pp. 399–400, and Norbert Lohfink, S.J. has written a book about
the implications of it (*The Covenant Never Revoked* [New York:
Paulist, 1991]) to which I am indebted. In the context of a mutual dialogue between Catholics and Jews, the Pope adopts the statement of
the German bishops, "Who meets Jesus Christ, meets Judaism"—and
he adds, "May I make these words my own." Speaking of the mutual
dialogue, he makes the following statement: "The first dimension of
this dialogue, that is, the meeting between the people of God of the old
covenant never retracted by God (Rom 11:29), on the one hand, and
the people of the new covenant, on the other, is at the same time a dialogue within our own Church, so to speak, a dialogue between the first
and the second part of its Bible." He continues immediately: "On this
the 'Directory for the Execution of the Conciliar Decree *Nostra
Aetate*' states: 'An effort will be made to acquire a better understand-

ing of whatever in the Old Testament retains its own perpetual values...since that has not been canceled by the later interpretation of the
New Testament. Rather, the New Testament brings out the full meaning of the Old, while both Old and New illumine and explain each
other.'"

The biblical reference is to Romans 11:29, "For the gifts and the
call of God are irrevocable." That statement is found in the three
chapters (Roman 9–11) in which Paul wrestles with the problem of
the failure of his compatriots ("beloved because of the patriarchs,"
11:28) to believe in Christ. There could hardly be a more tender and
loving regard for their belief than 9:4, "Theirs the adoption, the glory,
the covenants, the giving of the law, the worship, and the promises...." He denies that "God has rejected his people" (11:1), and he
confesses he cannot understand the mystery of it all (11:25), and he
can only finish on the note of the inscrutability of God and the divine
ways (11:33).

The words of Paul and of John Paul II are a true echo of the Old
Testament statements about the "merciful and gracious God" (Ex 34:6),
"who has compassion upon his children" (Ps 103:13). God's covenant is
as irrevocable as God's love. The vision in Isaiah 54 is never lost: "For a
brief moment I forsook you, but with vast love I bring you
back....Though the mountains be displaced and the hills be shaken, my
favor shall never leave you nor my covenant of peace be shaken, says
the Lord who loves you" (Is 54:7–10).

The *Nostra Aetate* document of Vatican II showed Christians a new
appreciation of their roots in the Old Testament, and of their relationship
with their Jewish brothers and sisters. Ultimately is there not one covenant
for Jews and Christians—the covenant never revoked by God? We are
both on the way to the eschatological showdown. Hence, there is no
supersessionism—fulfillment, yes, but not rejection or replacement.

Q. 94. How did Jesus view the Torah?

This question is hard to answer because the disputes of the early
church with Pharisaical Judaism color the Gospel narratives, and also
because Jesus did not display a one-sided view of affirmation or negation.
Doubtless he shared with his compatriots a deep reverence for the Torah

that God had given to Israel. This can be seen by his references to the law (in Greek, *nomos*) in all the Gospels save Mark (but cf. Mark 7:19). He orders the lepers to observe the ritual purification prescribed in the law (Mk 1:44). He is applauded when he singles out the heart of the law, the two commandments of love of God and neighbor (Mt 12:28–34). Precisely because of his appreciation of the law, he is able to create a new understanding of it that departs from that of the teachers of the day. With this departure goes the dawning realization of the populace that Jesus speaks with an authority that is unequaled in their experience.

In John's Gospel Jesus is described as being somewhat polemical and distant, in that he refers several times to "your" law (cf. 8:17; 10:34; see also 15:25). The most programmatic statement in John is 1:16–17, in which he writes that we have received from Christ's *pleroma* ("fullness"), grace upon grace, and he contrasts the law given through Moses with the grace and truth that comes through Jesus Christ. John is not even-handed here; he clearly regards the revelation through Christ as definitive and revealing of the Father. The Johannine Christ does not get involved with the evaluation of the law, except to claim that his opponents, although they search the Scriptures that testify in his behalf, refuse to believe in him (Jn 5:38–40).

Luke's view of promise and fulfillment is perhaps best exemplified in 4:16–21 (cf. 24:27, 44–45). He portrays Jesus preaching in the synagogue, reading (selected parts of) Isaiah 61 and proclaiming the fulfillment of the passage "today." The emphasis is on Jesus' mission to the poor and the outcast. He truly is "the one who is to come" (7:22). The attitude of Jesus is further manifested in the debates about the sabbath observance. Luke quotes him as saying "The Son of Man is Lord of the sabbath" (6:5) after he defends the eating of grain on the part of his disciples. He cures on the sabbath despite the opposition of many (Lk 6:6–11; 13:10–17; 14:1–6). Thus Jesus is portrayed as an interpreter of the law.

Q. 95. You have indicated how Jesus' attitude toward the law is portrayed in all the Gospels except Matthew. Does Matthew differ from the others?

The portrayal in the Gospel of Matthew is different, and not easy to reconcile with the others. It may represent an emphatic point of view of him and his community. It is worth treating separately because it is so detailed. A key text appears near the beginning of the sermon on the mount (Mt 5:17–20), "Do not think that I have come to abolish the law or the prophets. I have come not to abolish but to fulfill. Amen I say to you, until heaven and earth pass away, not the smallest letter or the smallest part of a letter will pass from the law, until all things have taken place....I tell you, unless your righteousness surpasses that of the scribes and the Pharisees, you will not enter into the kingdom of heaven" (*NAB*).

Immediately following this weighty statement are the famous "antitheses" (5:21–49). An antithesis is a literary form that sets up an opposition between two parts of a statement. It is formulaic: "You have heard (or the equivalent) but... I say to you." Three of these antitheses are usually described as sharpening or intensifying and interiorizing moral action (1, 2, 6; anger leads to murder, lust leads to adultery, love is not to be confined to a few, but shown to all). The other three antitheses abrogate items of the Torah: prohibition of divorce, abolition of oaths, dismissal of retaliation). Where he does not actually reject a given law, he radicalizes it, as the first group indicates. And the second triad shows that he felt equal to replacing or abolishing the law.

In Matthew 5:21 there is a bold comparison with established moral arbiters of the day: "Unless your righteousness surpasses that of the scribes and the Pharisees, you will not enter the kingdom of heaven." Jesus' denunciation of the scribes and Pharisees is found in Matthew 23:1–29, a series of woes. It is difficult to determine how much of this derives from Christ, and how much is the interpretation of Matthew and the community when the enmity between the Church and the established Pharisaism had hardened. It should be noted that this chapter is applicable in principle, even if the circumstances have changed, to the Christian community.

The meaning of fulfillment (5:17–18) is most difficult to articulate. What is meant by Jesus' fulfilling (and not abolishing) the law? Or that the smallest letter will not pass from the law until heaven and earth pass away? Little profit is to be gained by attributing these lines to Matthew himself or to the early Church. At least they were seen to be a legitimate expansion of Jesus' point of view. There are two ideas in vv. 17–18 that need further emphasis. The first is that Jesus upholds the law. This idea of fulfilling the law could have been affirmed by him against the opponents he claimed did not understand him. It also makes sense as post-Resurrection interpretation in the great early Christian debate of the binding force of the law, and also as a defense of Jesus against claims that he was opposed to the law (e.g., Acts 6:11–14). One may allow these possibilities, but they yield little certainty. I would suggest that the fulfillment of which Christ speaks is a part of the general fulfillment seen in the relationship of the two Testaments (cf. Q. 92). It is fulfillment as he understands it, moving on to another plane of motivation and activity, refusing any casuistry, radicalizing the laws that have governed the status quo. His fulfillment is really a transcendence, a going beyond in a faithful direction. It has to be seen in the light of the central message of God's imminent reign. Fulfillment of the law is the specific completion that he alone could give; it culminates in his person, for he is the prophet (Dt 18:15) to whom one is to listen (Mt 17:5).

The "passing away" of heaven and earth and the "accomplishing of all things" are in clear parallelism, and they seem to refer to the endtime, the eschaton that is described in Matthew 24:1–44. What about surpassing the righteousness of the scribes and the Pharisees (Mt 5:20)? On this W. Davies and D. Allison remark: "The tension between Jesus' teaching and the Mosaic Law is not that those who accept the former will transgress the latter; rather is it that they will achieve far more than they would if the Torah were their only guide" (*The Gospel According to Saint Matthew* [Edinburgh, 1988] 501–02). I have been trying to give a short summary explanation of the difficult passage of Matthew 5:17–20. Perhaps it is not possible in the light of the antitheses that follow.

Q. 96. Wasn't the early Church split on the issue of observing the prescriptions of the Torah?

That is true, and we can see this in Acts and in the letters of Paul. We must recall that the first community had to grow into a clearer definition of itself. The apostles are portrayed as going to the Temple to worship (e.g., Peter and John, Acts 3:1), as well as assembling for the breaking of the bread (Acts 2:46). The distinction between the Hellenists and the Hebrews within the community (Acts 6:1)—between those who spoke Greek and were more influenced by Greek culture and those who spoke Hebrew/Aramaic and were more at home in Jewish ways—is a harbinger of greater differences to come. One can sympathize with the Jewish converts to Christianity. Their way of life, and that of Jesus, more or less set the standards they thought should be observed. However, the situation was different for Greek converts and Jews from the diaspora. Peter raised the question (and solved it) by remarking about Cornelius the centurion and his group: "Can one refuse the water for baptizing these people who have received the Holy Spirit even as we have?" (Acts 10:47). Peter's dining with these "uncircumcised people" caused scandal at first, but a temporary understanding was reached (Acts 11).

But the issue did not disappear. The success of the first missionary journey of Paul and Barnabas precipitated a practical question: Was the Mosaic law to be imposed on the Gentile converts (Acts 15:6)? A compromise was reached at the insistence of James who was the leader of the (mainly Jewish) Christian members in Jerusalem. A certain pluralism within early Christianity was tolerated, as the early Church struggled to find its identity vis-à-vis the Jewish embryo from which it took its origin. The intensity of this struggle can be seen in Paul's description in Galatians 2:1–14 of his meeting with the "pillars," Peter and James, after his first missionary journey. Here Paul is recognized as entrusted with the Gospel for the uncircumcised as Peter is for the circumcised—a handshake seals this orientation. But when Kephas (Peter) separated himself from eating with Gentile Christians in Antioch, Paul "opposed him to his face" (Gal 2:11–14), and prevailed over Peter and the Jewish Christians from Jerusalem who had influenced Peter on this score. Paul relates these events because of the situation in the Galatian community where some are insisting on circumcision and observance of the law. However, it should be noted that the resolution of the problem given in the second chapter of Galatians is quite different from the solution proposed in Acts 10.

Q. 97. How would you describe Paul's attitude toward the Torah?

It is very complicated. He mentions the Torah (or *nomos*) almost one hundred times in the sense of the Mosaic law. The paradox is that he is both for it and against it. The two important epistles for the Pauline view are those to the Galatians and to the Romans. He presents different arguments in each, but the conclusion concerning the need for faith in Christ remains firm. One should also recall the background of the controversy in the early Church, briefly indicated above in Q. 96. A short, tidy answer to your question is perhaps not possible, but some important factors should be kept in mind in attempting to understand Paul on this topic.

From one point of view, "the law is holy, and the commandment is holy, just and good" (Rom 7:12). It is "the law of God" (Rom 7:25; 8:7). It is one of the great gifts the Lord made to Israel (Rom 9:4). Obedience to the law brings life (Gal 3:12, quoting Lev 18:5). On the other hand, "the law produces wrath—where there is no law, neither is there viola-tion" (Rom 4:15). Paul makes an addition to Psalm 143:2 to the effect that justification cannot be reached "by observing the law"—because the law merely brings consciousness of sin (Rom 3:20). He goes to great lengths in describing how sin has brought the (good) law into its employ-ment (Rom 7, especially vv. 7–8). Let these contradictory views suffice to show how complex Paul's understanding of the law is. They have to be seen against the background of the mystery of Christ.

Paul strives mightily to maintain that justification (or reconcilia-tion with God, or whatever synonymous phrase one may use) can be achieved only by faith in Christ, and not earned by observance of the law. This is at the heart of the two epistles, and utterly important in his theology. Jewish Christian preachers had urged Paul's converts to adopt certain Jewish practices, notably circumcision. This was the visible sign of observance of the law and inclusion in God's redemptive plan within Judaism. Hence Paul had to oppose all this in order to reveal the central-ity of Christ as God's definitive act of redemption. Our response, like that of Abraham, is faith in Christ (see Gal 3:6–18). Paul vigorously contrasts faith (in Christ) with "works of the law" (e.g., Gal 3:2, 5, 10). This particular situation calls forth polemics, and we are not given a calm and reasoned statement of Paul's views. The polemics described above in Acts may not be as evident as in the Pauline epistles, but the question is basically the same. For Paul the law is the teacher or "disci-plinarian" for Christ that we might be justified by faith, but we are no longer under the law (Gal 3:24–25).

In Romans 10:4 Paul writes that Christ is the "end of the law." In what sense is he the end? Does he exterminate the law as a life-giving source—or is he the end in the sense of goal? The first alternative would amount to supersessionism, which we have rejected above in Q. 93. Rather, Christ is the goal, as suggested by the context, in which righteousness is something that is pursued (9:30). For further details, see the treatment of this question by Joseph Fitzmyer in the *NJBC*, #82, 81–100. He goes on to correlate Galatians 5:6 ("faith working itself out through love") with Romans 13:8–10 where Paul quotes several of the Commandments and concludes that "love is the fulfillment of the law." His conclusion: "Only Paul has such a christological understanding of the law of Moses among NT writers" (#82, 98).

Q. 98. How would you compare the attitude toward the Torah in the epistle of James with Paul's view?

First, a few introductory remarks about this letter. It is pretty well agreed that, out of all the several characters named James in the New Testament, the James of 1:1 is intended to be the leader of the Jerusalem church, one of the "pillars" of the Church (Gal 2:9). Whether or not the work is pseudonymous is not important for our purposes. The author writes in a relatively elevated Greek style.

Despite the fact that this letter became a stumbling block in the controversy about "faith and works," it betrays little or no interest in the observances of the Torah, e.g., the need for circumcision or the ritual laws. His use of the term *nomos*, or law, is not frequent–only seven times. Twice he speaks of the "law of liberty" (1:25; 2:12), even calling it a "royal law" (2:8). What does this exalted language refer to? It would seem to be Christian morality. But of course this is derived from the Torah, and he quotes Leviticus 19:18 about loving the neighbor as oneself in connection with this "royal law." In the context he cites two of the commandments (relative to adultery and to murder), already part of Christian tradition. The same can be said of the references to the law in 4:11 where the law of charity is at issue. Basically James has no problem with the Torah. It is clear that he is not fighting the Pauline battle with Judaizers. He is correcting Christians who think that they have faith, but who do not live up to their calling. Their actions fail to conform to their words. Hence he writes in 2:14, "Faith by itself, if it has not works, is dead," and in 2:24, "A person is justified by works and not by faith alone." (How ironic that "faith alone" should appear only in James and *not* in Romans 3:28.)

Statements of this kind appear to be in conflict with the teaching of Paul, but ultimately it is because both men are speaking about faith from different points of view. In Romans 3:31 Paul denies that the Old Testament law is annulled by faith; rather he claims to be supporting the law, even though he writes in 3:28 that a person is justified by faith apart from the works of the law. Paul's point of view is that faith cannot be merited, cannot be won by observance of the works of the law; it is solely a gift of God (and, we might add, so also were the free promise of God to Abraham, and the covenant vouchsafed through Moses). But once a person has faith, what kind is it? What are the effects? It is a "faith working through love" (Gal 5:6). In contrast, James is very hard-headed and down to earth in his evaluation of a person who already has "faith," or claims to have it: "What good is it, brothers and sisters, if one says he has faith but does not have works? Can that faith save him?...Show me your faith without works, and I will show you my faith from my works" (2:14–18). The faith/works controversy of the Reformation period was complicated by the questionable "pious" practices and corruption in the Catholic Church, to be sure, and in the heat of controversy distinctions were difficult to make in theological matters. It is also true that James was coming at the Christian life from an angle that differed from Paul, and that accounts for the emphasis on works that Paul took for granted, but on a more theoretical level, as when he wrote about the gifts of the Spirit in Galatians 5:22–23, and when he warned that one will reap only what one sows (Gal 6:8).

Q. 99. What is the distinction between legalism and observance of law?

Usually legalism is understood in a pejorative sense, meaning a blind and strict adherence to the letter of the law without further ado. Or it may also be used frequently to describe the interpretation of a law that is contrary to one's own "reasonable" (?) and therefore "correct" (?) interpretation. Acknowledgement of the need to interpret law can hardly be denied. Positive law is essentially mutable, due to changing circumstances. One sees many examples of interpretation of the Mosaic laws within the Pentateuch. Within the New Testament there is the example of Christ in his understanding of the law concerning the observance of the sabbath or his interpretation of the law to honor one's parents (denouncing the use of *qorban* in Mark 7:9–12). Discrepancies in the interpretation of the Torah are really not new, as the differing tenets of the Sadducees and also of the Samaritans indicate. We know that Jewish interpretation of the Torah was not uniform in the intertestamental period. The writings of the Essenes of Qumran bear witness to these variations, and they are only the latest example that we have discovered.

The specter of "legalism" has haunted the Christian understanding of Judaism, especially the description of the devotion to the Torah in the post-exilic period. When one adds to that the well-known classification of 613 commandments in the Torah, the interpretation by a culture that is already inclined to be antinomian is warped. The basic thrust of the Torah places the commandments and statutes in the context of divine love. God loved and chose Israel out of love for the fathers (Dt 4:37; 7:8). Israel was far from being the largest of all nations; it was the smallest! It was not given the land of Canaan because of its merits or "integrity of heart" (Dt 9:5–6). The obligations of the covenant are thus in the context of God's love and grace. Obedience to the divine will is the *response* to the covenantal love. It need not be self-righteousness. Any individual or group can be self-righteous in their response—that is the way of human weakness and selfishness—but this is a distortion of nobler instincts.

In traditional Catholic theology there was (and it still operates) the principle of *epikeia*. This means that, in cases of positive law, one may act contrary to it by interpreting a situation according to the mind of the lawgiver when recourse to the lawgiver is not possible. The law itself may command or prohibit a particular action, but circumstances may render it inapplicable, and one interprets the situation by asking what the lawgiver would want done—and proceeds accordingly. *Epikeia* can be abused. At first sight it would seem to open the door to abuse and laxism, but it has stood the test of time, and it can be in the spirit of the law (cf. C. Curran in *NCE*, V, 476–77).

Q. 100. Is the Torah recognized in the new *Catechism of the Catholic Church*?

I did not find "Torah," but "law" occurs frequently enough. Parts of the Torah are prominent in the treatment of morality. Sections

2083–2571 give over one hundred pages to the Ten Commandments, used as a basis for moral action, good and evil; a great deal of natural law reasoning is employed. The Decalogue is seen as a kind of basic source for customary Christian morality. Its historical milieu is not regarded; more could have been done with the nature of idolatry, the imagelessness of the Lord, and the sabbath. In the chapter on prayer several sections (2568–2589) deal with prayer in the Old Testament, especially featuring the psalter. In the index a striking imbalance is shown in the absence of "covenant," in contrast to a reference to "concubinage." One has to be creative and look under other entries. Hence one finds under "Old Covenant" three items, and four under "Old Testament." The underlying attitude of the *Catechism* is that "the Old Law is a *preparation for the Gospel*" (#1964; cf. 1982). This attitude is enforced by frequent repetition throughout the work. Whatever truth that statement expresses, the result is unhappy if the Old Testament is blithely swept aside in the catechetical process. All this means a creative challenge to the individual catechist, who is properly informed about the Old Testament. The brief summary statement in section 1975 needs to be modified and filled out: "According to Scripture the Law is a fatherly instruction by God which prescribes for man the ways that lead to the promised beatitude, and proscribes the ways of evil." Until the Law is heard and understood by the Christian on its own level, it will fail to be a true preparation (see Q. 93).

Q. 101. Would you summarize a genuine Christian understanding of, and attitude to, the Torah?

Your question deals specifically with the law, but I think that my answer will be applicable to the entire Old Testament, and I don't think it will be peculiar to me; rather, it will reflect the views current among Catholic biblical scholars. I say this because of the 1993 document issued by the Pontifical Biblical Commission in Rome with a preface by Cardinal Ratzinger, entitled "The Interpretation of the Bible in the Church" (English translation from French, *Origins* 23/29, January 6, 1994, 498–594). There is a fundamental statement on p. 505: "The Church reads the Old Testament in the light of the paschal mystery—the death and resurrection of Jesus Christ—who brings a radical newness and, with sovereign authority, gives a meaning to the scriptures that is decisive and definitive....It ought not, however, mean doing away with all attempt to be consistent with the earlier canonical interpretation which preceded the Christian Passover. One must respect each stage of the history of salvation. To empty out of the Old Testament its own proper meaning would be to deprive the New of its roots in history" (p. 505).

This admirable statement appropriately distinguishes levels of interpretation: (1) the interpretation that the Church gives to the Old Testament (especially in the liturgy, one might add); (2) the meaning of the Old Testament before the Christian Passover—in other words, what the Old Testament means on its own level. I admit that there is a certain tension between these two levels. Surely a Christian can opt for a Christian meaning, where appropriate, thus interpreting the Old Testament in the light of Christ. My basic plea is that the Old Testament should not be swallowed up by the New; such a turn is detrimental to the Christian. If one insists that he or she wants to interpret the Bible solely from a Christian point of view, it would be better to simply read the New Testament, instead of distorting the Old Testament by reading it *only* as preparation. The revelation of God deserves better. Moreover, concentration on the New Testament may involve more problems than one bargains for. The literal historical character of the New Testament is distinct from the development in meaning that has taken place during the centuries the Church has lived with it.

To conclude: the literal historical meaning of an Old Testament text is also the primary Christian meaning, the meaning that a Christian interpreter (or, indeed, a Jewish interpreter) thinks is intended by the author for all readers, Jewish or Christian. It need not be Christological. Rather, taken on its own level, the Old Testament has much to teach the Christian. Secondly, one must be alert to the particular and limited perspective of the New Testament as regards Christ and Christianity. There is a tension between the proclamation of Peter in Acts 4:12 (salvation in no one else but Christ), the attitude of the epistle to the Hebrews (e.g., 8:13, the old is obsolete), and such statements as 2 Timothy 2:1–4 (God the Savior desires all to be saved). The New Testament has to be interpreted in the light of history (including Vatican II). The New Testament writers spoke primarily to the realities of their day; they were not laying down propositions about the mysterious plans of divine providence for the totality of humankind in all future generations. Vatican II acknowledged as much in its statements regarding the value of non-Christian religions (see, e.g., the Constitution on the Church, *Lumen Gentium*, chap. 2, paragraphs 14–16). Rather, while both the apostolic Church and Christians today proclaim that Christ is the Savior of all, *how* this is worked out over the centuries among the millions of God's children remains a mystery to us. But we can find the clues to the great love of God for the whole world already unfolding in the foundational books of the Torah!

INDEX OF PROPER NAMES AND OF SUBJECTS TREATED IN THE QUESTIONS

(The numbers listed below refer to Questions, not to pages.)